Alice in France

The World War I Letters of
Alice M. O'Brien

Edited by Nancy O'Brien Wagner

MINNESOTA
HISTORICAL
SOCIETY PRESS

The publication of this book was supported though a generous grant from the Eugenie M. Anderson Women in Public Affairs Fund.

www.mnhspress.org

The Minnesota Historical Society Press is a member of the Association of American University Presses.

Manufactured in the United States of America

10 9 8 7 6 5 4 3 2 1

♾ The paper used in this publication meets the minimum requirements of the American National Standard for Information Sciences— Permanence for Printed Library Materials, ANSI Z39.48-1984.

International Standard Book Number

ISBN: 978-1-68134-026-5 (paperback)
ISBN: 978-1-68134-027-2 (e-book)

Library of Congress Cataloging-in-Publication Data

Names: O'Brien, Alice M. (Alice Marie), 1891–1962, author. |
Wagner, Nancy O-Brien, 1973– editor.
Title: Alice in France : the World War I letters of Alice M. O'Brien /
edited by Nancy O'Brien Wagner.
Description: St. Paul, MN : Minnesota Historical Society Press, 2017. |
Includes bibliographical references and index.
Identifiers: LCCN 2016054090 | ISBN 9781681340265
(paperback : alkaline paper)
| ISBN 9781681340272 (e-book)
Subjects: LCSH: O'Brien, Alice M. (Alice Marie), 1891–1962—Correspondence. |
World War, 1914–1918—Personal narratives, American. | World War, 1914–1918—
France. | World War, 1914–1918—Women. | Women volunteers—France—
Correspondence. | Americans—France—Correspondence. | Women—Minnesota—
Correspondence.
Classification: LCC D640 .O18 2017 | DDC 940.53/1 [B] —dc23
LC record available at https://lccn.loc.gov/2016054090

This and other Minnesota Historical Society Press books
are available from popular e-book vendors.

Alice in France
is set in the Scala typeface family.

Book design and typesetting by
BNTypographics West Ltd., Victoria, B.C. Canada

Printed by Versa Press, East Peoria, Illinois

IN MEMORY OF
Thomond Robert O'Brien

Contents

Preface and Acknowledgments

The first person who died in World War I was a woman.

In our shared memories of the Great War, it is a man's story. Through romantic lenses, we picture black-and-white doughboys with bowl-shaped helmets tipped at rakish angles, peering fiercely over the edges of their mud trenches, or dashing male pilots stepping into their fragile propeller planes and zooming off into the sky. With clearer eyes, we see men's bodies ripped apart and strewn across muddy fields. Gas masks, bloated horses, crippled tanks. We recall the cruel, glorious, patriotic, brave, or meaningless deaths of millions of men at Verdun, at the Somme, at Passchendaele, in the Marne, at Ypres. It was a war of men directed by men: Ferdinand Foch, Erich Ludendorff, Douglas Haig, Alexei Brusilov, John Pershing. Those memories are true, but that is not the full story.

When women are included in the story of World War I, they are most often placed passively on the side of the stage. In the United States, we describe how they filled their roles as patient and virtuous wives or mothers, gamely waving farewell, bundling up care packages, writing letters, wrapping bandages, and knitting scarves. In Europe, women hold these roles and also occasionally step forward when the spotlight falls on their status as stunned victims of horrific violence or weary refugees fleeing the chaos. Those memories are also true, but that is not the full story.

Occasionally, we have brief scenes where women become true actors in the story—interacting with the people around them and affecting events—though often at a small scale. These stories have been boiled down to images of a chaste Red Cross nurse, a spunky ambulance driver, or the dangerous and sexual spy Mata Hari. Indeed, those memories are also true, but that is not the full story.

From the death of Archduchess Sophie Ferdinand on June 28, 1914, women were always a part of the story. Not just as witnesses or victims, and not just as nurses, ambulance drivers, or spies. Women worked and volunteered directly in the war as clerks, cooks, doctors, bookkeepers, telephone operators, searchers, laundresses, canteeners, social workers, typists, supply truck drivers, nurse's aids, recreational volunteers, stenographers, secretaries, and chemists and in other roles. They participated in the broader war economy as factory workers, farmers, shopkeepers, and cab drivers. Military rules and social customs prevented women from serving as soldiers on the battlefield, but as the war progressed, women pressed up against these conventional boundaries, testing to see what new roles they could step into.

For European women, this exploration was directly tied to a personal motivation to defend their fellow citizens and their homeland. Their fathers, brothers, and sons were dying in the battles; their cities, towns, fields, and homes were being overrun and endangered. They stood to lose, personally, if the enemy was triumphant.

For American women, the threat was more remote—both in distance and in theory. For the first years of the war, Americans clung to the idea of neutrality. As President Woodrow Wilson stated, "The United States must be neutral in fact, as well as in name." This approach was pragmatic, and it was based on the varied ancestry and sympathies of Americans, the economic dangers of picking sides, and the belief that the political entanglements and historic enmities of Europe were not our problem. As the war developed, Americans' sympathies began to swing to the Allied side. The invasion of Belgium, the sinking of the *Lusitania* and other ships, and the release of the Zimmerman telegram (in which Germany encouraged Mexico to declare war on the United States) hardened Americans' opinions against Germany. When Wilson requested that Congress formally declare war and join the Allies on April 2, 1917, most Americans supported him. On April 6, Congress approved, and the United States entered the war. A propaganda campaign helped convince many of the remaining skeptics, arguing that US intervention was needed to stop German atrocity and autocracy and to make the world a freer and better place.

Within six weeks after the United States entered the war, approximately 73,000 men had volunteered to join the armed services, which had stood at about 121,000 at the start of 1917. The government quickly realized it would need more numbers and enacted the Selective Draft Act on May 18, 1917. With the threat of a draft looming and the influence of an effective propaganda campaign, around 2 million men volunteered for service, joining the 2.8 million who were drafted.

American women were under no obligation to serve in the war. They were not drafted, they were not personally endangered, and indeed they were culturally discouraged from entering the masculine arena of war. Regardless, they did serve. In fact, despite these barriers, thousands of American women volunteered to work in France. While military leaders were uncomfortable with the presence of women in masculine jobs, pragmatic considerations outweighed their discomfort: each woman who served as a driver, mechanic, or accountant freed up a man who could serve in the trenches. In addition, the women were good at their jobs, and they often worked for free.

Minnesotan Alice O'Brien was one of these women who volunteered to serve in France in World War I, initially as a mechanic and later as an auxiliary nurse, canteener, and supply truck driver. It is hard, a century later, to truly understand her motivations. Her letters show her strong sympathies for France and her deep hatred of the Germans. She was part of a group of adventurous women who traveled together and volunteered together. Her fascination with and knowledge of cars gave her a particularly valuable skill in the war zone. Her strong personality, problem-solving skills, good humor, and stamina made her well suited for the challenges she faced. But even with those attributes, her choice to volunteer for France gives one pause. While her privileged position colors her accounts in sometimes surprising (and amusing) ways, her status does not diminish her accomplishment.

As the daughter of a successful lumberman, Alice's wealth and status meant she could do almost anything a woman could do at that time. Many of her contemporaries spent the war years maintaining their social lives and starting families while also volunteering locally and raising funds for the Red Cross. Like the female protagonists in the novels of F. Scott Fitzgerald (a fellow St. Paulite, just five years Alice's junior), these women were well insulated from the rough travails of life—particularly the dangers and discomforts of places like a war zone.

Instead, Alice willingly chose to go to France as a war worker and press against the boundaries of what was allowed to women. Like thousands of other American women, something drew her to step forward onto the stage and into a role that placed her in the greatest event that happened in the world at that time. Indeed, though our memories of her and her contemporaries have faded, she was a true actor in this history and deserves a part in the story.

～

Alice O'Brien was my grandaunt. Stories of her larger-than-life experiences, personality, and impact continued to circulate throughout my early years, even though she passed away a decade before I was born. "Aunt Alice" remained a strong figure in my family's memory, particularly through the stories of my father, Tomy O'Brien Sr. When my father died in December 2007, we mourned the loss of not only his own memories but the last strong connection to Alice. A few months later, cleaning out the attic, my mother, Alvina O'Brien, and I came across a sheaf of papers: Dad's efforts to transcribe Alice's letters from France. A few weeks later, we found the letters themselves. Reading Alice's words directly inspired my imagination and this project.

Thanks to that discovery, the support of the Twin Cities Chapter of the American Red Cross—particularly Carrie Carlson-Guest and Lori Bents—and the funding provided by a Minnesota Historical and Cultural Heritage Grant, made possible by the Arts and Cultural Heritage Fund, I was able to develop the article "Awfully Busy These Days: Red Cross Women in France during World War I," which was published in *Minnesota History* magazine under the wise guidance of Anne Kaplan in spring 2012 and was awarded the Solon J. Buck award for best article that year. With the encouragement of Ann Regan, the article and the letters grew into this history.

In addition to my mother, other family members and friends came forward with additional resources about Alice and her life. Robin Brooksbank offered a diary that William O'Brien had written about a family trip in 1913 and many additional photos from Alice's time in France. Kate O'Brien painstakingly transcribed and shared the William O'Brien diary, which brought insight to Alice's personality. Terry O'Brien Jr. allowed me to dig through his collection of items, resulting in the unearthing of photos and letters from Alice. Alice's legacy of family loyalty and generosity is particularly evident in these cousins. Jo Wright, the daughter-in-law of Alice's friend Margaret Ames, shared her family's archives and photos relating to the efforts of the American Fund for French Wounded. Spencer Kellogg Neale, the son of Alice's friend Doris Kellogg, shared a photo and stories of Alice, who was his godmother.

Local historians know how lucky we are to have the resource of the Minnesota Historical Society. The staff of the library there is incredibly helpful and generous in their advice and support. The staff of the St. Paul Public Library, the Minneapolis Public Library, and the Andersen Library at the University of Minnesota were also incredibly helpful, and I appreciate all they do. Within the Minnesota Historical Society, a broad group collaborated to strengthen, support, and promote this effort: Shannon Pennefeather, Alison Aten, Randal Dietrich, Danielle Dart, Brian Horrigan, and Matthew Prediger—the finest bunch of pros I've ever seen. Margaret Lee, a great friend and awesome historian, also provided critical support during an early stage. Sara Yaeger, Caragh O'Brien, Laura O'Brien Smith, Chris Wells, and Anne Lippin all offered sage editorial advice and emotional cheerleading as needed.

None of this would be possible, however, without the incredible work and effort of our bevy of babysitters, Eileen Lewis, Leah Tornquist, and Lara Avery, or the sweet inspiration of their charges, Nolan, Franny, and Zoë. Finally, a great sea of gratitude goes to the man who makes it all work—or at least makes it all fun—my husband, David O'Brien Wagner.

A Note on the Editing

Alice O'Brien wrote frequently to her family during her time in
France. Forty-eight of her letters home have survived, as well as two
additional letters to her family from friends. A majority of letters
were typed on her portable Corona typewriter, though some were
handwritten, too. My father, Thomond O'Brien, was the first to work
with Alice's letters, and he made the initial pass at transcribing and
organizing them. I scanned his document, then used optical character recognition software to translate it into text. The combination
of that process and the original transcription introduced many typo-
graphical errors, which required correcting. A handful of letters had
been overlooked, and I transcribed and inserted those. Alice's letters,
unfortunately, were not always dated, and most of the envelopes they
came in were disposed of. Using hints within the letters and cross-
referencing them with the letters written by her companion Doris
Kellogg, I have placed them in order and assigned likely dates. Following military orders, Alice did not name her locations, so I have
also added those for clarity.

Alice wrote to her family, so she did not bother to refer to people
by their full names. Through research, I was able to identify many of
the people she wrote about, and information about them is included
in the footnotes.

Alice was well educated for the time, and her letters are grammatically clear. I corrected obvious typos: thime to time, thave to have, thir to their, diners to dinners, then to them, clothers to clothes, sark to dark, and the like. However, to maintain Alice's voice, what appears to be unconventional spelling remains. Rumour, harbour, aeroplane, and tho reflect the spelling standards of the time and have been kept. Camauflaged, unexpressibly, rightaway, and kaki are too charming to correct.

Alice in France

ONE

Alice Before the War

In the predawn darkness of April 7, 1918, Alice Marie O'Brien and her companions were summoned to the deck of the SS *Rochambeau*. There, twenty-six-year-old Alice huddled in her steamer chair, her lifebelt resting nearby, and watched as the dawn begin to glow in the eastern sky, silhouetting the gunners who anxiously scanned the waves for signs of a submarine attack. As the ship heaved beneath her and the cold wind whipped by, Alice's mind turned to the life that awaited her in France. She was headed to war, certain to face the dangers of life in a war zone: illness, discomfort, homesickness, and possibly bombs. Alice considered those uncertainties and, with characteristic aplomb, noted she was "primed and ready for work."

As the daughter of the successful Minnesota lumberman William O'Brien, Alice had no need to work at all, let alone for no pay and on the front lines of a war in a foreign land. Like many women of her class, she could easily have stayed home, raised money, and wrapped bandages. But like the thousands of other women who served in France, Alice had a sense of bravery, adventure, and patriotism leading her across those dangerous waters and into a war zone.

Alice's love of adventure and her courage had been apparent for years. Growing up in St. Paul at the turn of the century, Alice lived with one foot in the rougher, western world of outdoor adventure and lumber camps and one foot in the genteel, eastern world of art, literature, and finishing schools.

Alice's parents were William O'Brien and Julia Mullery. William had grown up in Taylors Falls, the son of a lumberman, and had learned the trade as a scaler, walking through the woods and estimating the board feet the forests would make. Julia had grown up in St. Paul, and her father was also involved in the lumber trade. In the late 1800s, the O'Briens and Mullerys went into business together, first logging in northern Minnesota and eventually expanding into Florida, the Carolinas, and the Bahamas. In 1890, Julia and William married in Hinckley, and Alice was born on September 1, 1891, in St. Paul. Her family was living in White Bear Lake when her brother William John (Jack) was born in 1895, but had moved to St. Paul by the time her brother Robert was born in 1902.

By 1905, the family had moved to 1034 Summit Avenue, a new home constructed by William and Julia for their young family.[1] Two servants, an English immigrant named Mary Lawler and a Minnesotan named Margaret Bauer, helped the family.

Alice was first educated in St. Paul: she studied at the Convent of the Visitation School, then at Miss Backus' School. At the Backus School, she studied languages, science, literature, history, art, expression, physical education, violin, piano, dancing, household arts, and horseback riding.[2] Many of the daughters of St. Paul's wealthier families attended Backus, and Alice socialized with them in and out of school. She began a particularly close friendship with her classmate Marguerite Davis.

As was common at the time for young women in her peer group, Alice traveled east for further education. She attended the Bennett

---

1. This property is just west of what is now the Minnesota Governor's Mansion, at the corner of Summit Avenue and Oxford Street.

2. *St. Paul Pioneer Press*, 1 April 1968.

Like many other daughters of St. Paul's industrial leaders, Alice attended the Backus School. She stands near the center of the circa 1909 photo in a white shirt, framed by the open door at right.

Finishing School for Young Women in Millbrook, New York, and graduated from there in 1911. There she met the daughters of eastern industrialists, such as Doris Kellogg from Buffalo.

Soon after her graduation from Bennett, the first hints of Alice's unconventional life began to appear. While many of her classmates and friends married and had children, Alice found herself pulled toward adventure, travel, automobiles, and suffrage. Among her contemporaries were other like-minded women, and Alice developed close relationships with them that continued for decades.

The summer after her graduation from Bennett, at just nineteen years old, Alice and a group of friends, including Doris Kellogg, drove Alice's roadster to explore the American West. Just two years earlier,

Alice Huyler Ramsey had become the first woman to drive across the United States. With three women passengers, Ramsey traveled the dirt tracks from New York City to San Francisco, arriving after forty-one days.[3] Stories of women like Ramsey must certainly have inspired Alice.

By this time, Alice had already developed her skills as a mechanic and driver. Family history recounts that her father taught her to drive by going up and down the driveway of her home, then up and down Summit Avenue. She taught herself about motors by taking apart her family's car and putting it back together again.[4] Images from this era show her posed behind the driver's wheel of a Franklin roadster with her friends nearby. Their long dresses stop just above St. Paul's dirt street.

Outside of the city, the roads were even worse. Pictures from this era show Alice and her companions leveling out the ruts with shovels. Doris Kellogg's son Spencer Neale reports that during the 1911 trip west, Alice and her companions' car was stuck on an isolated road in Arizona. The travelers were becoming alarmed when they noticed a group of Native Americans on horseback on a hill above them. The riders galloped down the hill and, to Alice and Doris's relief, simply dismounted and helped to push the car out.

Following a more conventional path in the spring of 1912, Alice, along with Doris Kellogg and other Bennett friends and a teacher chaperone, Mrs. Sherwood, traveled to northern Africa and Europe for a four-month tour. Alice's letters describe her journey as she passed through Algiers, Egypt, Italy, Austria, Spain, Gibraltar, Granada, and France. As one might expect, the letters focus on her experience as a tourist, though one telling detail appears over and over. Near the end of many letters, Alice repeats this refrain: "Did Mama

---

3. Scharff, *Taking the Wheel*, 76–77.
4. Alvina O'Brien interview, 6 September 2016.

In spring of 1912, Alice (center) and three friends from the Bennett School traveled to Egypt and Europe with a teacher, Mrs. Sherwood.

order a new touring car?" "Did you order a new car? Don't omit letting Mr. Seagraire know that I want mine delivered on May first if you don't come abroad. Maybe we could have it delivered in Buffalo and tour home in it." "Don't forget the Pierce." "Did you order my car?" "Give my love to all and don't forget to order my machine if you haven't already ordered it. I would love to see it at the dock in N.Y. along with some other charming faces."[5]

5. Alice O'Brien to Robert O'Brien, postcard, 28 January 1912; to Mama (Julia O'Brien), undated letter from Assouan; to Mama (Julia O'Brien), undated letter from Athens; to Mama (Julia O'Brien), undated letter from Florence; to Mama (Julia O'Brien), 20 March 1912—all in Alice O'Brien Letters, Alvina O'Brien Archive.

As described by historian Virginia Scharff, the birth of the automobile coincided with the birth of the progressive woman.[6] While
Ford and Olds were tinkering with their engines and developing
new designs, educated and wealthy women were beginning to claim
their rights to unrestricted travel and public spaces. The car industry, born in the dirty mechanical spaces of factories and garages, was
initially very masculine. The first horseless carriages were difficult to
drive and dangerous at worst; dirty, dusty, and cold at best.

For Alice, and for other women during the early 1910s, owning
and driving a car were political statements. During the Progressive
Era, when women were pushing to expand their access to education, careers, and the ballot, the car was literally broadening their
horizons. While many wealthy men and women initially relied on
chauffeurs to operate the cars, "modern" cars with enclosed cabs and
easier ignition made driving much more enjoyable for both male
and female drivers. Apparently, Alice was enamored with cars before
the more user-friendly designs were available. Pictures of Alice from
this period show her bundled up to drive her outdoor-cab car, no
small challenge during a Minnesota winter. The debate about the
propriety of women driving cars would continue for the next few
years. In 1914, the magazine *Motor* sponsored an essay contest about
the question "Do Women Make Good Drivers?"[7] Alice's behavior
answered clearly: yes.

On January 16, 1913, Alice, her mother Julia, her father William,
and her brother Robert (Bob) headed to Wilson City, Grand Abaco,
Bahamas, to visit one of William's lumber operations, the Bahamas
Timber Company. Also accompanying them were Alice's aunt Marie
Mullery O'Connor and Albert Lammers, a Stillwater lumberman
and partner of William's. Her aunt Nora Mullery and brother Jack

---

6. Scharff, *Taking the Wheel*, 4, 9.
7. Scharff, *Taking the Wheel*, 31.

later joined them. Nora and Albert struck up a romance on the trip and married a year later. On the trip, Alice was an enthusiastic explorer, rowing to nearby Lynyards Cay Island in hopes of catching a shark. A few days later, with the assistance of their captain, she was able to shoot her shark. On the trip, a fortune-teller read her palms and foretold a long series of happy events for her. On March 30, Alice and her brother Robert departed for St. Paul. Her parents and the rest of the party stayed until April 25.[8]

Back home, Alice returned to cars and suffrage work. At times, her two passions combined, as in 1914 when she was photographed in her car promoting a lecture by Christabel Pankhurst, the famous and influential English suffragist. As head of the political education committee of the Women's Welfare League (which also included her friend Marguerite Davis), Alice was responsible for engaging Miss Pankhurst and introduced her at the event.[9] Later, Alice recalled that she had been paralyzed with stage fright.[10] If so, it would have been one of the few times she hesitated at a challenge. Her courage and confidence appeared early in life. As the newspaper account put it, Alice was "a younger society girl who is known as an expert woman motorist. She is interested in all out-of-doors sports and is equally skillful at golf, tennis, cross-country riding and hunting."

Alice's interest in and expertise in the outdoors was remarked upon by many who knew her. The following year, Alice and Marguerite were once again making the news, this time for their ability to handle a gun. They, along with Mrs. Harold P. Bend, were "three of a group of St. Paul society women, who have gone hunting this

8. William O'Brien, "A Brief Account of Trip to Wilson City; January 16th to April 25, 1913," transcribed by Kate O'Brien, 2010, Robin Brooksbank Archive.

9. *St. Paul Pioneer Press*, 6 December 1914.

10. *St. Paul Pioneer Press*, 4 February 1934.

Alice was an experienced outdoorswoman, known for being a good shot.

fall. All three considered exceptionally good shots."[11] Accompanying photos show the women aiming their guns.

For Alice, the next few years were spent traveling to visit friends, assisting her father with business matters, tinkering with cars, and enjoying her first houseboat, the *Ripple*. Alice's love of boats and watercraft was a strong characteristic throughout her life. Early photographs show her canoeing in quiet lakes and streams. Around 1917, Alice's father sold his house on Summit Avenue and bought a

11. *St. Paul Pioneer Press*, 21 November 1915.

summer house overlooking the St. Croix River in the community of Marine on St. Croix (then known as Marine Mills). With deep roots in the valley and family nearby, the O'Briens felt at home. Alice loved the scenic environment and became a lifelong fan of the St. Croix valley. For the next few years, the family kept a house on Holly Avenue in St. Paul as a base for the fall, winter, and spring months and moved to Marine for the summers.

~

When World War I broke out in Europe in 1914, Alice's allegiance to France would have been unquestioning. Though Woodrow Wilson strove to maintain US neutrality in the first years of the war, people such as Alice were politically and culturally sympathetic to France— especially after having traveled there. In St. Paul, efforts to support the French quickly sprung up. Alice's friend Elizabeth (Betty) Ames and her family organized the local chapter for the American Fund for French Wounded (AFFW), a group that helped provide medical supplies and support to France. Similar smaller volunteer groups popped up throughout the country, such as the American Huguenot Committee and the American Relief Clearing House (ARCH). Larger, established organizations such as the American Red Cross, YMCA, and YWCA began offering support, too.

For people who wanted to be more actively involved in the war efforts, there were plenty of opportunities to volunteer. In France, groups of expats formed ambulance units and sponsored hospitals. The investment bank Morgan-Harjes funded an ambulance corps, which was called the Morgan-Harjes Section. The bank paid for the automobiles, and the drivers were volunteers from the United States. Richard Norton organized a similar group, and the two were combined under the American Red Cross in December 1915 and became known as the Norton-Harjes. Initially, the American men who rushed to volunteer as ambulance drivers were alumni of Ivy

League colleges and East Coast prep schools such as Harvard, Yale, Princeton, St. Paul's, and Phillips Academy.[12] As the first American men to volunteer for the war effort in France, these men used their backgrounds and resources to build up their organizations and scope out their preferred roles. Alice later noted to her brother, "The Red Cross has plenty of Bank presidents in France and a lot of them have been here for a long time so have first shot at the interesting jobs."[13]

Students and alumnae of women's colleges were equally determined to support the efforts in France, even more so once the United States entered the war in April 1917. The cultural gender expectations of the times, however, significantly limited opportunities. While male volunteers were recruited for ambulance positions, women volunteers were steered toward softer roles like canteening, clerical work, social work, nursing (where qualified), or working as a "hello girl" (a member of the woman's telephone unit of the US Army Signal Corps). Smart, politically connected, well-organized, and privately financed groups of women from Wellesley, Vassar, Radcliffe, and Smith struggled to establish independent units in France. In most cases, the groups were quickly consumed by larger organizations like the Red Cross. Others were able to stake out and defend territories that they could independently manage.[14]

The efforts of the Red Cross were staggering. In France alone, from July 1, 1917, to February 28, 1919, the Red Cross established 551 stations from which they offered service. Twenty-four of these stations were hospitals run jointly by the Red Cross and the US Army. These hospitals had 14,800 beds, served 91,356 patients, and had just 1,457 deaths. In addition to the hospitals, the Red Cross also ran twelve convalescent homes for soldiers and organized reconstruction

12. Hansen, *Gentleman Volunteers*, xiv–xvii.

13. Alice to Jack, 31 July 1918.

14. Schneider and Schneider, *Into the Breach*, 72–73.

and rehabilitation efforts for crippled and disabled men. They had emergency depots of medical supplies for the American army and medical supply depots for French hospitals. They also produced and supplied all necessary splints, nitrous oxide anesthetic, and oxygen for the army. In addition to the medical support, there were canteens. The Red Cross operated 130 canteens, serving over 6 million meals and 12 million drinks. These canteens operated on the front lines, along the lines of communication, and at aviation camps, evacuation hospitals, and metropolitan centers. Beyond that there was recreation and welfare service, hospital service, hospital farms and gardens, moving pictures for hospitals, photography of graves for grieving families back home, civilian relief, relief of French soldiers' families, children's relief (including hospitals, clinics, canteens, expositions, and adoption assistance), and anti-tuberculosis relief.[15]

American women like Alice who wanted to volunteer in France had a variety of options beyond the Red Cross: approximately fifty-two American and forty-five foreign service agencies and war organizations.[16] At the time the United States entered the war in 1917, the roles of each of these groups was still unclear. In February 1918, the Red Cross's official jurisdiction over the sick and wounded was confirmed. Other relief agencies could offer recreational, educational, and religious support to soldiers. Both the Red Cross and other groups could continue to offer relief to civilians, refugees, and soldiers.

While the Red Cross was the biggest game in town, it wasn't the only one. In the late winter of 1917 and early spring of 1918, when Alice and her friends Marguerite Davis, Doris Kellogg, and Genevieve Washburn were evaluating which organization to enlist with, they were probably attracted to the AFFW due to its smaller, less bureaucratic nature. Through her familiarity with the Ames family,

---

15. American Red Cross, *The Work of the American Red Cross*, 49–64.
16. Schneider and Schneider, *Into the Breach*, 50.

WHAT?
ARE YOU GOING TO DO
FOR YOUR COUNTRY?

Sewing · Linen room work
Surgical dressings · Laundress
Dietician · Cook · Waitress ·
Packing · Shipping · Cleaning
Interpreter · Translator
Clerical service · Typist
Stenographer
Telephone operator
Telegraph operator
Special · (not classified above).

HELP
The American Red Cross
ENLIST NOW AT

The American Red Cross used patriotic images and phrases to recruit women to serve both on the home front and overseas. Their images promoted independent female figures, while the sample job descriptions remained firmly traditional. Alice's efforts as a mechanic, auxiliary nurse, canteener, and supply truck driver would have been "not classified above."

Alice was likely assured that they would be given significant responsibilities at the AFFW. Alice, Doris, and Marguerite signed up to be mechanics and Genevieve as a driver—roles which would never have been offered to them in the Red Cross. Genevieve's family even committed to sending a car over.[17]

Though the organizations were different, the women who signed up for them were generally cut from the same cloth. Most volunteers agreed to work for no pay. The state department required that female volunteers could not have a father, son, husband, or brother in the armed services. In the Red Cross, office workers had to be between twenty-eight and thirty-five years of age, and similar rules applied to other positions and in other organizations. Preferably, volunteers should also have some knowledge of French or Italian.[18] These restrictions largely limited the volunteer pool to those without spousal obligations or significant financial needs—unmarried, educated, upper-class women.

Like many others, Alice coordinated her application with her friends. Applying in groups of two or even four friends was common, and the letters between the women tell us much about their friendships.

Having applied for and been accepted by the AFFW, Alice would then have needed to get approval from the war department. The application requirements were demanding: recommendations, four "loyalty" letters from prominent people who would vouch for an applicant's allegiance, interviews, vaccinations, inoculations, proof of birth in the United States (no German or Austrian ancestry allowed), then passports. By March 1918, Alice had completed the process. She was ready to head to France.

17. Alice O'Brien to Mama, Dad and All, 26–28 June 1918.
18. Red Cross Foreign Service, "Qualifications necessary for women stenographers, bookkeepers and clerical help," in Dee Smith Papers, Minnesota Historical Society.

TWO

The War in Spring 1918

Alice and her family must surely have fretted as the news from France reached Minnesota's newspapers that spring. By March, Germany's advantage was clear. The previous year, Russian Tsar Nicholas II had been forced to abdicate, and Russia had collapsed under a series of revolutions. With the country in turmoil, Russian troops began to withdraw from the Eastern Front in the fall of 1917. In December 1917, Russia reached an armistice with Germany. With the conclusion of the war with Russia, Germany could shift its attention—and a million battle-tested soldiers—from the Eastern Front to the Western Front. It was a race between the arrival of the German reinforcements and the American ones. German General Erich Ludendorff was determined to win the race.

Just before dawn on March 21, 1918, as a dense white fog shrouded the land, the Germans launched their first of four planned attacks in Ludendorff's Spring Offensive, an aggressive strategy to force their way through the Allied trenches near Amiens and toward Paris. For five hours, the Germans pounded the trenches with six thousand guns, releasing a barrage of shells and gas.[1] Over a million shells were

---

1. Cruttwell, *History of the Great War*, 506.

fired: one in four was gas.[2] After the bombs ended, and before the Allied troops could recover, an elite group of German soldiers known as storm troopers began pushing through the defenses. Armed with light machine guns, flamethrowers, and grenades, the small detachments of storm troopers sliced deep into the Allied trenches.[3]

As the storm troopers advanced, regular German troops followed them, and soon the Allied soldiers were cut off from each other. The tactic was novel on the Western Front and extremely effective. The Allied line buckled and retreated. Within a day, Germany was using an enormous cannon called Big Bertha to drop bombs in Paris. Desperate to respond to the German advance, the Allies took the long-overdue step of appointing Ferdinand Foch to command all Allied armies on March 26.[4] By March 30, the Germans had advanced to approximately sixty miles from Paris, severed a railway to the city, and taken 80,000 prisoners and 975 guns.[5] The battle line had shifted much closer to the city, and the Allied troops were struggling to defend and hold their positions.

As word of Foch's appointment and the retreat of the Allied lines reached the United States, Alice and her friends completed their final preparations. Alice and her mother, Julia, headed to New York City and stayed briefly with her aunt Lorene Mullery Brown and her family. On March 29, Alice and her mom likely stayed at the Brevoort House, a hotel on the corner of Fifth Avenue and Eighth Street.[6] It is hard to know how Alice's parents felt as she prepared for her departure. From Alice's letters, it is clear they had mixed emotions. Alice later thanked her mother, saying, "you have been great about

---

2. Winter and Baggett, *The Great War*, 289.

3. Cruttwell, *History of the Great War*, 494–95.

4. Cruttwell, *History of the Great War*, 510.

5. Hart, *The Real War*, 371.

6. Alice's letters from the boat are written on Brevoort House stationery, suggesting she might have taken some from that hotel on a recent stay.

letting me go without a fuss," but also described hearing that "Dad was still saying that I had no business in France."[7] At the age of twenty-six, Alice was old enough to press for her own desires, but it is likely she would not have gone if her parents had strongly objected, and could not have gone if they had cut off the purse strings.

On March 30, 1918, Alice and her friends made their way to the crowded pier where the SS *Rochambeau* was docked. At the entrance to the Custom House, she embraced her mother and Aunt Lorene. She stepped into the building, stopped to wave farewell to her family through the window, then turned to head to her next adventure: France.

---

7. Alice's letter to Mama (Julia O'Brien), 30 March 1918, and letter to Mama (Julia O'Brien) and All, 19 July 1918.

Alice O'Brien's Letters from France

1918

[Onboard the SS *Rochambeau*[8]]

Dear Mama—

On Board & comfortably settled. It took us just one hour & a quarter to get thru the Customs but we got thru O.K. They took nothing from us and I only hope we'll have the same luck on the French side.

Dode[9] and I are together and Mugs[10] and Genevieve.[11] The boat is packed with men and women, all in Uniform, and mostly men. We, in civilian clothes, are far in the minority.

The Boat seems very comfortable and substantial,—our cabins light & comfortable.

---

8. The SS *Rochambeau* was a French transatlantic ocean liner that traveled between Bordeaux and New York City. It was owned by the *Compagnie Générale Transatlantique*, or the "French Line," as it was commonly called. During the war, the company shifted its vessels to the war effort, using them as warships and hospital vessels and for transportation for troops and war workers. The French Line's patriotism cost them, though: approximately one-third of their ships were destroyed during the war.

9. Doris Kellogg.

10. Marguerite Davis.

11. J. Genevieve Washburn.

It is so interesting to see all the people and wonder how they got here and what they are going to do. 180 men of a Southern Regiment are onboard, lots of other Military, 30 or 40 Salvation Army men and women, 180 Red Cross men and loads of others. Several Naval officers walking around & looking important and we have guns fore and aft with French Gunners. Our camouflage is Blue, Tan and Grey put on in Stripes, Squares & Triangles—awfully queer.

Mr. Bobbet[12] is on board & on deck with us but have seen no one else. He is in Red Cross Uniform; Lots of French *officiers* around—well—so long—you have been great about letting me go without a fuss—and Thanks for the laundry.

Loads of love to you,
Alice
Good Bye & Love to Lorene, Rob & Children[13]

~

[31 March 1918]
On Board second day out.

Dear Mama, Dad and All—

You see we are already using our Corona but it is so much smaller than the typewriter that I am used to that it is going to take a little time to get on to it. The boat is wonderfully comfortable and crowded to the gunnels. I could tell you quite a lot about the military on board

---

12. Frederic William Bobbett (1869–) was an accountant from St. Paul.

13. Alice's aunt Lorena/Lorene Mullery and her husband Robert A. Brown and children were living in New York during this time. Alice stayed with them just before her departure.

but I am sure it would be censored so I guess you will have to wait until I get home to hear all the really exciting things that happen. We had our places at the lifeboats assigned to us today and then had a lifebelt drill. It was very calm and uneventful but the fat people in lifebelts were very diverting. We have already begun to practice our French on the best employees, they don't speak English so we have to. Mugs distinguished herself last night by calmly walking up to the Steward, she was looking for her trunk, and said "Steward, where is my leg?" He laughed and proceeded to show her as best he could when she realized that she had made some sort of horrible mistake so returned to the cabin, told us about it and we laughed half the night.

Today has been beautiful, calm and warm, we have been on deck all day without coats, just basking in the sunlight. The passengers are mostly, or almost entirely, made up of war workers and it is a unique boatload when you think that we are all here, together, with the same idea in mind and all on the way to France on the same mission.

Well, I must go below and wash before dinner. Will save this letter and add to it from time to time. I hope this weather lasts, it is beautiful and warm.

Al.

~

Fourth day out [2 April 1918]

Here I am sitting out on deck in my steamer chair and leather coat, just as cozy as can be, the sun shining brightly and the ship comfortably rolling in a light wind. Mugs and Genevieve are walking the deck a thing I seldom do, and Dode is hanging over the rail staring at the Polish soldiers. We are going to be convoyed thru the war zone because we have troops on board, six war ships are to meet us Friday and see us to Bordeaux. We get war news by wireless every day and I think we are going to beat the Germans to Paris after all.[14] I will add a postscript to this letter and mail it from Bordeaux.

We are enjoying our supply of food immensely as the ship fare does not include sweets. After every meal we adjourn to our cabin and have a piece of one or the other of the cakes. We are already eating war bread[15] and there is not a pound of butter on board. I am rather glad because we might just as well get used to it first as last. Always fruit for dessert but nothing else. They never use sugar if they can help it.

My cold is completely gone, Dode's also, the fresh warm air was bound to do it. We go to bed early, there is nothing else to do. The boat is so crowded that you cannot possibly get a chair in the Salon and the decks are inky black. No light on deck since we left New York. All portholes covered, and soldiers on guard to see that no one violates the laws. Mr. Bobbett innocently lighted a cigarette on deck last night and a soldier appeared out of the darkness in the wink of an eye and told him to put it out. The ship does not even carry a light on her forward mast but does all her navigating by wireless.

The Salvation Army is certainly on the job, singing hymns every minute, organizing bible classes and spreading sweetness and light

---

14. By April 2, 1918, the initial attack of the "Spring Offensive" was stalling. The German troops had advanced substantially, but it was difficult territory to support with fresh troops and supplies. It had been a brutal, bloody battle, with 255,000 casualties on the Allied side and 239,000 on the German side.

15. Food conservation for the war effort was encouraged on the home front and even at sea. Sugar and wheat were particularly needed for Allied soldiers and civilians in Europe. "War bread" was made with less flour and substituted corn syrup for sugar and shortening for butter.

all over the place. Poor Souls, it is a shame that they are not more appreciated. They have five women and three men on board who are going to work with the American Army in the army camps in France. Judging from the number of canteen workers, Y.M.C.A. men, etc, I think every man in the Army will have an uplift.

Love,

Al.

I wear my identification card

∽

Sunday Afternoon—ninth day out [7 April 1918]

Dear Family—

Here we sit, Doris and I bundled up in our steamer chairs enjoying the world as best we may. We are right in the middle of the war zone but our promised convoy has yet to show up.[16] It is probable that

---

16. During the first two years of the war, German U-boat submarines frequently targeted and destroyed military ships, merchant ships, and civilian ships in the Atlantic Ocean—whether enemy or neutral. Their torpedoing of the ocean liner *Lusitania* in May 1915 and the subsequent deaths of 1,198 passengers, including 128 Americans, helped form Americans' attitudes against Germany. After President Woodrow Wilson strenuously complained, the Germans resisted attacking nonmilitary ships for a while, but it was too effective as a strategy to sacrifice. In January 1917, Germany announced it would sink any ship it saw on the high seas, and in March 1917, Germans sank five American merchant ships. American outrage helped tip the scales and led Congress to declare war on April 6, 1917. By mid-1917, the Allies had developed the strategy of employing convoys to prevent submarine attacks. Grouping twenty or more ships, including warships, into convoys allowed them to better see attacking submarines and to more effectively counterattack.

we are being convoyed but that they are out of sight and it is also probable that we have nary a convoy at all. Everyone on deck has their life belt beside them, the nervous ones are straining their eyes for periscopes. The French gunners fore and aft are pacing up and down beside their guns which are loaded and ready, the lookout is in the top crows nest on the forward mast, he looked like a human fly climbing up the rope ladder, there are eight guards around the deck all armed with powerful spy glasses, everybody knows their life boat number by heart and where to go and stand for orders in case of trouble, all the life boats are supplied with beef, crackers, and kegs of fresh water and are slung over the side in place and down level with the deck, all ready to jump into. The Women get in first before the boats are lowered and the men go over the side and down the rope ladders. All the preparations make me realize that we are really here but if it were not for that I do not think that I would ever think of the old submarines. Some people have been sleeping fully dressed, out on deck but the zone does not prevent us from getting in about twelve hours good sleep every night in our little cabins. We are all wonderfully well except for Genevieve's cold. I have not the slightest sign of my cold left, this is the truth. I feel like a million dollars and get fatter every day.

We expect to reach the mouth of the river some time during tomorrow night, anchor until dawn and then go up the River to Bordeaux, about fifty miles. Huge prison camps line both sides of the River so we will see our first sight of the war before landing. Most of the prisoners and all of the interned German civilians are in the Bordeaux camps. We have had a wonderful passage and a good rest so are primed and ready for our work. A man on board has crossed the Atlantic over thirty times and said that he has never had a trip to compare with this one. We are always lucky and if tomorrow, our last day, can touch today we will have had a one hundred per cent perfect trip. No one has been seasick, not even Genevieve who gets sick every time she gets on Lake Superior. Mr. Bobbett had his third inoculation last night so spent a miserable night and looks pretty pale and wan this morning. I am so glad that I have had everything. Have heard it rumored that we would be quarantined 24 hours before we land but doubt the truth of it. They might hold the troops but I think they will let the passengers thru.

I can think of nothing else to write now and I see the deck steward arriving with our afternoon tea so think I will imbibe. He brings beef bouillion [*sic*] every morning at eleven and tea at four and in between times we go below and nibble at our own supply and then go to meals and eat as much as we can get. Think I had better look up Dode. She disappeared some time ago and as all uniforms fascinate her she is as apt to be with a deck hand as with one of the dashing French officers on board.

I will not write again from the ship, unless something exciting happens, but will mail this in Bordeaux and write you another as soon as we get to Paris. I am going to number my letters, this will be No. I—and in addition will number the sheets so you can tell if any go down on the way over or if the censor takes any sheets out. I suggest that you do the same.

Lots of love,
Al

Please send this to Jack[17] because I have nothing new to write and don't want to write the same thing over again.

Just a last line before I mail this letter—It is now 5:30, afternoon, of our last day out and we will sight land in about 3 hours. I guess nothing thrilling will occur in that time so it is safe to seal the letter. In case of taking to the boats I was going to carry it in my pocket so you would have a real Souvenir. We had a thrilling morning.

---

17. William John (Jack) O'Brien, Alice's brother.

Everyone slept fully dressed last night, orders from the Captain, and we arose at dawn as we were told that a Submarine attack was most likely at that hour, if at all. It was wonderful to see the guns & gunners silhouetted against the sky. The Bay of Biscay is always rough, called the Graveyard of the Ocean, and it was fun to stand on deck and feel the boat heave under you and, of course, the possibility of a lurking Submarine gave an added zest to the briskness of the morning.

Received the candy from Teta & Bob,[18] thanks so much, also the address from Auntie Marie.[19]

Love again,
Alice

We are not convoyed but passed a fleet of freight boats going in the opposite direction that were accompanied by 3 Submarine Chasers.

Love to everyone—Mae, Val, Helen, Charles,[20] John,[21] the O'Briens,[22] the Lammers,[23] Teta, Auntie Marie, the Browns,[24] and, anyone else you see.

~

---

18. Alice's aunt Teresa (Teta) Mullery and Alice's brother Robert (Bob) O'Brien.

19. Alice's aunt Marie Mullery (1859–1935).

20. Alice's uncle Valentine Mullery, his wife Mae, and their children Helen and Charles.

21. Likely Alice's uncle John Mullery.

22. Alice's relatives on her father's side.

23. Alice's aunt Nora Mullery Lammers and her husband Albert J. Lammers.

24. Alice's aunt Lorene/Lorena Mullery and her husband Robert A. Brown.

[9 April 1918][25]
American Y.W.C.A. Hostess House
Hotel Petrograd, 33–35 Rue Caumartin, Paris 8e

Dear Auntie Marie and All—

See where we are! We have had a thrilling time already. Twelve hours before reaching the mouth of the River the Captain received word from Shore that Submarines were in the vicinity so we changed our course, went due North and then came sneaking along the coast into the Harbor. It was thrilling, everyone in lifebelts, etc., but we did not know our real danger until it was past. We anchored at the mouth for the night and the next day came up to Bordeaux. Never have you seen or heard of such a welcome as the old Ship received on her triumphant entry—People lined the banks and shouted, waved handkerchiefs & aprons, sang, screamed, all the whistles tooted themselves into a frenzy, Soldiers stood at attention, flags waved—oh!—everything happened. I cry to think of how emotional it was. We had dinner in Bordeaux with Mr. Paige[26] & Mr. Bobbett and took the night express for *Paris,* our objective. Arrived this a.m., met by American Red Cross, hustled into a bus and advised to come here until we made arrangements for permanent lodgings. It is immaculately clean, an old Hotel taken over & run by American women for American girls, comfortable & warm, and what do you think we had for breakfast—Bacon & Eggs & Butter. Hotels are not allowed to

---

25. Alice didn't know that her arrival in Paris coincided with the start of the second attack in the Spring Offensive. Using the same tactics as they had in March (see pages 17–18), the Germans pressed north from their new salient against the Allied troops, striving to reach the ports of Calais, Boulogne, and Dunkirk.

26. Likely Walter C. Paige (1871–), a YMCA volunteer from Houston, Texas.

serve butter in Paris but they have a special permission here as all guests are war workers. We have a nice room & could live here for $2.50 a day, including a good Breakfast and Dinner. We think that this is too far from our work or we would probably stay. However, we shall see.

Paris looks just the same, except that the lack of traffic seems queer and so many of the shops are closed. We have already noticed how black prevails—so many widows.

Well—love to you all—don't worry about me. We are comfortable and safe. France is not at all exercised over the outcome of the war. Perfect confidence in the outcome.

Love again,
Alice

~

[11 April 1918]
[9 Rue de la Grand Chaumiere,] Paris

Dear Mama and all—

We have been in Paris for four days and so many things have happened that I can not settle down to start to write about them all. In the first place, the authorities have passed all sorts of regulations about gasoline which materially curtails the operations of the motor service of the A.F.F.W. There are only seven cars in their Paris garage now, all the rest have been sent out to depots and operate around the district that the depot is in. It looks as tho there was not going to be enough work for the Fund to do to have them keep us busy as a motor repair unit. They want us to stay with them until some of the cars that are on their way over get here and then drive them but we do not particularly fancy running errands around Paris so do not know yet just what we will do. Major Olds,[27] of St. Paul, is with the Red Cross here and is quite the big bug of the place and they have been very nice to us. Mrs. Olds called the first day we arrived and invited us to dinner. They have an apartment here and we went over and had a very nice time. It was quite like being in St. Paul and I did wish that you could see us sitting there, Betty Ames[28] also, just as cozy as we could be and having a wonderful dinner, in spite of all the tales we were told in the States that we would starve to death, etc. Major Olds is trying to put thru a measure to remove all the men for the automobile service of the Red Cross here in Paris and environs and put women in their places and if so, wants us to drive Red Cross cars. If that does not go thru he wants us to run a canteen in southern France but whatever we do we will be hard at work before you get this letter. We are so glad that we are here and are sorry that we ever listened to the tales about there being too many American girls in France. There is loads of work for everyone to do and it is really a wonderful thing to feel that you are going to help in your own small way to win the war.

We have loads to eat and it is not as expensive as we thought it would be. We stayed for the first three days at the Y.M.C.A. hotel, had comfortable rooms and good food but it was right in the center of the city and too noisy so we moved and are now at 9 Rue de la Grand Chaumiere. It is run by a Frenchwoman, is immaculately clean and so cheap. We get our room and breakfast for about thirty dollars a month and have the rest of our meals out.

---

27. Robert Edwin Olds first helped establish the Home Service Department for the St. Paul Chapter of the American Red Cross before he traveled to France. His wife, Rose W. Olds, also worked in France for the Red Cross.

28. Elizabeth (Betty) Ames, later Elizabeth (Betty) Ames Jackson.

A few of the limited American Fund for French Wounded cars outside the organization's office.

The long-range gun has dropped a few shells into Paris for the last three days but no one thinks of paying any attention to it.[29] It does not throw a bad shell, only dangerous in an eight foot circle wherever it strikes and Paris is so big that it seems more like a mosquito bite than a gun. We went thru our first air raid last night. We were just getting into bed at ten o'clock when we heard the alarm given and a second later heard the first bombs explode. Only a few machines got thru the defense of Paris and they succeeded in dropping some bombs before they were driven out [but] not many. We looked out at the sky and saw it flare up from the reflections of the

---

29. The long-range gun was located seventy-five miles away near Laon, and the shells took more than five minutes to arrive. A spotter called Paris when the shell was launched, giving Parisians time to sound the alarm and take cover. Cruttwell, *History of the Great War*, 531.

bursting bombs and every now and then would see a twinkle which looked like an unusually large star but which we found later to be the bursting of a shrapnel shell from one of the defense guns. Before long the noise died down and we saw the searchlights sweeping the sky for Boche machines[30] Not long after the all clear signal was given and we returned to our beds and slept soundly until nine this a.m. We are living in thrilling times and I would not give up the last few days for all the money in the world.

I am going to cable to you tomorrow. It is rather discouraging trying to cable or write because I hear that many of the letters are lost and that the cable companies are too rushed to give attention to private cablegrams but all we can do is try.

Love to all and I do hope that you won't worry about me. I so often wish that you could see how safe, comfortable and happy we are. I am getting so fat that I will have to diet if it keeps up.

Love to all,
Al

∼

[~15 April 1918]

Dear Mama and all—

This is letter no. 3 to 436[31] and one to Auntie Marie on the side. I just heard that a boat was sailing tomorrow so thought I would drop this note on the way home.

---

30. *Boche* was a disparaging term used to describe Germans during the war.

31. 436 Holly, the address of her parents in St. Paul.

COURTESY OF JO WRIGHT

Women volunteering at the American Fund for French Wounded transformed bolts of cloth into bandages and linens for hospitals.

We are at the Alcazar[32] and have been packing all day. They are having a rush on account of the big offensive and are shipping loads of stuff to the Hospitals and have asked everyone to help for a few days.[33] We are all well and very comfortable, work hard but love it.

---

32. The Alcazar D'Été was a café and dance hall that was transformed into a staging space for the American Fund for French Wounded.

33. The "big offensive" that Alice lightly mentions here was the second effort of the Germans' Spring Offensive, named "Georgette" and begun April 9, the day she arrived in Paris. This famous push nearly annihilated the Portuguese Second Division and challenged the British army along the north edge of the front near Calais. The British troops were stretched out and weak and too far for French reinforcements to quickly reach. The situation was dire. British Field Marshal Sir Douglas Haig famously encouraged

There is plenty of food in Paris but I would appreciate some candy—everyone craves for it as you get so little sugar.

Love to all—if you could see things here you would not worry about me—young & old working hard and never a worry about anything.

Love to all,
Alice
Did you get my cable?

~

21 April 1918

Dear Family—

It seems ages since I've heard from you as we have not yet received any mail. The *Espagne* got in to Bordeaux a few days ago so we expect some mail from her and do hope that we'll get it as we are all homesick for news from America. We are glad that we came when we did because we were talking to Keith Clark,[34] who came on the *Espagne,* and she said that they had a wretched trip, cold and very stormy, luck seems to be always with us.

---

his soldiers on April 11: "Many of us are now tired. To those I would say that victory will belong to the side which holds out the longest. . . . There is no other course open to us but to fight it out! Every position must be held to the last man: there must be no retirement. With our backs to the wall and believing in the justice of our cause, each one of us must fight on to the end. The safety of our Homes and the Freedom of mankind alike depend upon the conduct of each one of us at this critical moment." Cruttwell, *History of the Great War,* 517, 518–19.

34. Keith Clark (1879–1951) was a female writer for the *St. Paul Dispatch* and later became a professor at Carlton College.

Paris seems at times almost as remote from the war as New York but at other times, during Gotha[35] raids or long range cannon bombardment, it seems as tho we were almost at the front but our dug-out, instead of being a hole in the ground, is a little room on the third floor back, of a French pension. Every morning at seven thirty the maid comes and lights a fire in our little fireplace and at eight o'clock returns with hot water and our breakfast. We get up, partially dress and have our "dejeuner" before the fire. I have a delicious large cup of chocolate and a hunk of war bread but Dode, always afraid that her figure will get the better of her has coffee. Then we dress and go to work. The garage is only a block away on a funny quaint little street only a block long and more like a courtyard than a street. The Red Cross has sent us a Ford chassis to assemble, just to see what we can do I think, so we start at it tomorrow morning. I do not know whether there is going to be enough work at the Garage to keep us busy but we are going to take a swing at it and try it out and if it seems a waste of time we are going to get released from the A.F.F.W. and do canteen work for the Red Cross. They are crying for American girls to work in canteens along the American line of communication from the ports to the trenches, that does not mean that they are under fire, they never allow that. We have met loads of Americans, army and Red Cross people, and if we were free we would have so many jobs to choose from that our heads would swim. Every one in France is counting on America to win the war and it looks as though it were going to be a long job. The French women do what they can but most of them have not been trained to be independant [sic], as the Americans have, so are hampered in their war work.[36] The class that is helping most are the women of the poor

---

35. Gotha was a type of heavy bomber biplane used by the Germans.

36. After less than two weeks in France, Alice's opinions of French women and their gender roles were not based on much evidence. Oddly,

who you see doing almost all the work that was done by men, running shops, street cars, subways, porters in the stations, driving wagons and doing all sorts of odd jobs. We did not expect to see a taxi in Paris but you can get one almost any time. Of course, they are all falling apart and the drivers are octogenarians but they seem to get you there somehow. There are also a few cabs around town but they are pretty sad looking as all the horses that can pull a load have been sent to the war. The people who have been here right along say that a noticeable change has come over the city, over seven hundred thousand people have left since the raids and bombardment started, there is practically no traffic in the streets, no gay crowds on the Bois, no stunning cars or turnouts, no gay windows, half of the cafes closed, no lights on the streets at night and wounded soldiers everywhere. It is tragic to see them so mutilated. You see so many wounded that the abnormal becomes normal and a man without a leg or an arm is considered lucky or "bien blesse" they say here, meaning happily wounded. Most terrible of all are the ones with distorted faces and we see so many of them. The hospital in which they make over faces is in Paris so most of the soldiers with face wounds come here to be fixed up. If their faces are terribly shot away they remodel wax masks from old photographs and it is ghastly to

---

though, her impressions had some truth to them: before the war, the French feminist movement was rather small—especially when compared to the broader, more popular movements in the United States or Great Britain. During the war, like their counterparts in the United States and other allied countries, French women served directly as war workers in munitions factories, as replacement workers in general jobs, and as agricultural workers. They also served the military as nurses, drivers, and clerical workers. All this while their men were being conscripted and dying in battle and the war was being fought on their native land. Unlike in the United States, however, the war did not create a significant or permanent lift in French women's status: they did not receive the vote until 1944. Darrow, *French Women and the First World War*, 3, 9.

In addition to assembling AFFW cars, Alice and the other mechanics
maintained the cars.

see their sad eyes looking out of smiling wax faces. The French are
wonderful, nothing can daunt their spirit, they are as staunch now
as when they started on this four years of hell, they always rise to the
occasion and fill in the gap just as they did in this last offensive when
the British line broke.

We went down to the Gare du Nord, the railroad station, the other
night to visit the canteens of the Red Cross and the A.F.F.W. The
refugees were pouring thru from the evacuated districts, all they
own in the world packed in bundles and carried on their backs. Most
of them were old people or children and looked so weary and tired
that it would wring your heart to see them. I talked to one woman
who was evacuating for the second time and was carrying three
children, twins one month old and a little girl aged two. One woman
showed me where the sabres of the Germans had cut great gashes
across the scalp of her child, a little boy about three, when they took
the town they lived in about a year ago. The A.F.F.W. furnishes

clothing and shoes to those that need them and the Red Cross gives them bread, cheese and hot chocolate. They are so simple and grateful that it is a pleasure to do things for them and it takes so little to make them happy, at least for the time being. One Old Lady came in with a granddaughter, neither of them had had anything to eat since early morning and it was then ten thirty P M, she looked so sad and tired that I thought she would never smile again but after three cups of chocolate she brightened up and took a new lease on life. The Red Cross is doing wonderful things—give them all the money you can spare.

I will write soon again and in the meantime I do hope to hear from you. Please write often, I need news from home for the good of my morale.

Love to you all,
Alice

We get our uniforms tomorrow and shall be photographed for the benefit of relatives. I think that you will be able to stand the shock.

～

[23 April 1918]

Dear Bob—

I planned about the fifteenth of April that on the seventeenth I would write you a birthday letter but by the time the seventeenth arrived I forgot all about it. However, I hope you had a happy birthday and I will bring your birthday present home with me. Perhaps by that time I will have a german [*sic*] helmet for you.

The war news over here looks pretty blue but the French still have the utmost confidence that it will all come out well in the end. It

Like many women volunteers in France, Alice was extremely proud of her uniform.

Doris (Dode) Kellogg, 1918.

looks like a long job for America and everyone over here is counting on two or three more years. The streets are filled with soldiers of every kind and if you walk along one of the large Boulevards at a crowded hour it makes your head swim to try and keep track of the uniforms. It gives me a thrill every time I see a dusty Packard or Pierce truck go down the Rivoli packed with American boys.

We met Mrs. Ladd[37] who was a New York sculptress before the war but who is now working for the Red Cross in the department for the relief of mutilated soldiers. She makes masks for the soldiers whose faces have been blown away. Some of the men are so badly mutilated that they have to be fed thru tubes and they have no features left at all. She makes a very light-weight mask for them, reconstructed to look as they did from old photographs they give her. Some famous French surgeons have been working at the same thing but Mrs. Ladd has been so successful that the Red Cross is going to put a lot of money in her department and do things on a large scale.[38]

Dode, Mugs and I went to Notre Dame to high mass this morning, it was a beautiful service but quite sad to see such a large percentage of the population in mourning. The wonderful old rose windows are being removed to keep them safe from the air raiders and all the famous carving is covered with sand bags.

We had another raid the other night but it was a very tame one. We heard the Siren just at midnight so hurried into our coats and a

---

37. Anna Coleman Ladd was actually a resident of Boston. She and her husband, Dr. Maynard Ladd, both traveled to Paris in December 1917 to work for the Red Cross.

38. By the end of 1918, Ladd and her assistants had produced 185 masks, according to the *Smithsonian* article "Faces of War: Amid the Horrors of World War I, a Corps of Artists Brought Hope to Soldiers Disfigured in the Trenches," by Caroline Alexander (February 2007). The Red Cross itself recorded the number of portrait masks to be 94. American Red Cross, *The Work of the American Red Cross*, 55.

few warm things and ran down into the cave. Everyone here calls a shelter under the ground a cave but they are nothing but cellars and very ordinary ones at that. We sat around and yawned and blinked at the candlelight, listened to the guns popping in the distance and when the all clear went off we went up stairs and to bed again. We are so accustomed to the cannon that it does not even wake us up. It has been very quiet for the last few days, perhaps it is on the bum. The last time they dropped a shell it hit a stable and killed ten horses.

Our uniforms came last night and we feel like three stiff soldiers but it is very nice to have them because everyone in Paris is in uniform. Especially the English and Americans.

We have just finished assembling a Ford Chassis for the Red Cross and it was a triumphant moment when it purred out of the Garage in perfect order. The Red Cross is terribly in need of motor drivers and canteen workers and it looks as though we were going to be pressed into service at one of the two trades. We rather like the idea of a canteen and will know which we are going to do some time this week. I received a letter from Al Warren[39] he is an instructor for the time being at some Artillery school and will get off to see us before long. We heard that John Abbot[t][40] has been reported missing. Isn't it too bad. I am afraid that it means that he is gone because the report here is that in the first few days of the offensive the Germans didn't bother to take any prisoners.

Tomorrow is the day for new bread tickets so we all have to pace over to the police station of our district and swear to a million various things and will then be handed our tickets for the coming month.

---

39. Alvah Hall Warren Jr. (1887–1964).

40. John Steele Abbott (1883–1959) was born in Ramsey, Minnesota, and captured in Lagnicourt, France, on March 21, 1918. He was later released and married a British woman in England in 1919 before returning to live in St. Paul.

Marguerite Davis, Genevieve Washburn, Doris Kellogg, and Alice O'Brien.

The bread restrictions do not bother us at all, in fact, we never eat our full allotment but I have never seen people eat as much bread as the French do. No wonder America has to conserve to feed them.

Well, we are just about to go over to Henriette's to dinner. It is a tiny little restaurant where you get wonderful things to eat for a franc or two a meal. I love to [eat] French cooking when I can avoid the garlic.

Dode sends her love with mine, to all the family,

Love,
Al

~

2 May 1918

Dear Lorene[41] and All—

Yours was the first letter to arrive from America and I tell you it was good to get it. It only arrived yesterday so you see how slow mail is in getting here. We have been hanging around like lost sheep waiting from mail to mail for news from home but now that it has started to come thru we will not be such a long time without it again. I also received a letter from Mama written from New York so American [sic] does not seem as far away as it did a few days ago. I can easily understand why the warring governments want people to write to the soldiers, it really does bring up your morale to receive a letter.

We are beginning to feel quite settled in Paris although our work is still rather indefinite. You see the Red Cross is taking over almost everything in France and I would not be supprised [sic] to see them swallow the American Fund but whether they do or not they will

---

41. Alice's aunt Lorene Mullery.

certainly control the Motor Service as we have to depend upon them
for all gasoline, supplies, etc. The negotiations between the Fund
and Red Cross have been going on for some time and are almost
settled so we will know in a day or so just where we stand. With the
Red Cross there will not be any immediate need for girls to do the
garage work as they have brought over so many American mechanics but they are figuring on taking the drivers off of all the Red Cross
cars around Paris and putting girl drivers in their places because
they are short of camion[42] drivers at the front and the girls could
release just as many men for active service. If they need us to drive
we will do it but we have a secret hankering to get into canteen
work. They are bringing Americans in by the thousands and starting
new canteens all along the lines of communication and need many
American girls for the work. They are crazy to get the three of us and
would send us all to the same canteen so we may be leaving Paris
before long. At any rate we are anxious for the situation to clear up
so we will know just where we do stand. In the meanwhile we have
not been idle. The Red Cross asked us if we could assemble a Ford
for them. We said "Sure, send it along" and the next day they did
send it, in a box, placed it carefully on the garage floor and left. We
had a lot of fun putting it together and great was our interest when
we got it all set up, cranked it and it started. We jumped aboard and
ran it around the block, hanging on to the thing by our teeth because
there was not a body on it and the French people looked at us as
much to say "Three crazy Americans." The Red Cross man came
over and inspected it, found everything O.K. and said that as long
as we got that far with it why not go a bit farther and make an automobile out of it so we took the body off of an antidiluvian [*sic*] wreck
that stood in the corner for months, put it on the new chassis and
then went for another ride. We finished this forenoon, there was

---

42. French for "truck."

nothing else to do so we took the rest of the day off and went on a spree. We donned our spanking new uniforms, took a taxi and made for the center of town, had luncheon on one of the Boulevards, walked out the Champs-Élysées and then took a fiacre[43] and drove to the Bois. It was a beautiful, warm sunshinny [sic] afternoon and I feel that it has been one of the days I shall always remember. The very Spirit of France seemed to be in the air and hovering around the Arc de Triomphe, saying to the Germans: "Do what you may, I shall never die." There were soldiers everywhere, French, English, Scotties, Algerians, Americans, Portugese [sic] and even a few Russians, and all the color of their uniforms blended into the fresh green of the Spring. It is sad to see the wounded sitting on the benches, so many of them without arms or legs or, what is even worse, their faces horribly mutilated and looking as though they had given all they had for the cause and had settled down to calmly suffer the rest of their lives away. Yet, every day, we see crowds of young boys marching away to the trenches singing and laughing as their's [sic] was the happiest lot in the whole world. The French are truly wonderful but they can not hang on forever and everywhere you hear the same question "How long is it going to take America to get here?" Everyone expects the U.S. to stand the brunt of things from now on and I guess things are still far from being over.

We are living in the Latin Quarter and what few artists that are left in Paris live around here so it is quite interesting. We live in a typical French house, thru a little court and then up three flights of clean slippery stairs to our little room. A French bonne wakes us every morning by bringing up our chocolate, lights our fire and then goes singing down the hall. We heard today that Trilby[44] posed in the

---

43. French for "carriage."

44. Trilby was a main character in the popular 1894 book of the same name by George du Maurier. In the novel, Trilby was an artists' model and a laundress.

Cars driven by American women for the AFFW, Paris Alcazar East.

art academy across from us so the neighborhood had taken on still another interest. There are numerous good, little cafes in the district and we have our luncheons and dinners at some one of them every day.

Things have been very quiet lately, no air raids and the cannon falling so far away from us that we don't even hear it. However, all the stars are out tonight so we will probably be spending most of the night in the celler [*sic*]. When we hear the alarm we get up and slip into some warm clothes, grab our money, letter of credit and our papers and make for the cave. We usually talk to the natives for an hour or so, listen to bombardment and then go back to bed. It really isn't half bad and at times like these it is really nice to have something definite to do such as going to the cave. Not like when the cannon falls, just stand around and wonder where the next one is going to hit.

Well, guess I'll retire now—thanks so much for writing and write soon again—love to all the Browns and the rest of the family.

Love again,
Alice

This is in red ink because the other tape is worn.

⌁

3 May 1918

Dear Jack—

It is so disconcerting to write to you because I am never quite sure where to send the letter but I think I will send this to St. Paul and if you are not there they will forward it to you.

We have been in Paris for three weeks but have not really settled down to work yet but everyone has the same tale to tell, there is loads of work to do and not half enough people here to do it but things are so mixed up and rushed that all newcomers just have to wait and gradually settle into things as they find them. We have assembled a Ford for the Red Cross and mounted the body from an old car on to it so we feel that we have made one car for the service even if we do not do anything else in the line. It looks as though the Red Cross wanted to take all the men off of the Paris cars and replace them with girls and if that is so I think we will be more valuable as drivers than as mechanics. I sort have [sic] feel that we would like to get into the canteen service of the Red Cross and if we do not do it now I think that we will have a swing at it before we leave to America.

I got a letter from Al Warren the other day. He is south of here at an artillery school and wants us to go down for a week end [sic] if he can not arrange to get to Paris so [I] guess we will see him sooner or later. Have seen the Taylors several times and see Mr. and Mrs. Olds quite often so we feel in touch with St. Paul.

Paris is full of American officers and soldiers, waiting for equipment I suppose. The important thing seems to be for America to get stuff over here, there is no use sending soldiers if they have not got anything to fight with. Practically all the guns that Americans are using on the line now were manufactured in France and all the American aviators are flying French planes. It is about time that we would get some of our own stuff over. There are only two Liberty Motors in France and only one of these works and they started manufacturing them a year ago. Henry Ford or some one must be asleep on the job.

Two days later—[5 May 1918]

Everything is settled—we went to Mrs. Lathrop[45] and told her that we did not want to wait around and wait for the cars to arrive from America before we had work to do and that the Red Cross was crying for American girls to do canteen work and that we wished to resign and take up the other work. She rather held on to us at first but finally saw our point so tomorrow morning we go to the Red Cross and sign up as canteen workers. If, at the end of three months time, the A.F.F.W. finds that it needs us in the garage we will finish our six months with them. We are crazy to get started on this new work and to know where we will be sent. They have canteens all over France some north of here and some to the south, we will know tomorrow where we are going and I will write Mama tomorrow night. The work is not at all dangerous, even if we are sent north of Paris because they always evacuate canteens under bombardment which is more than I can say for Paris. However, Paris has not been

---

45. Isabel Stevens Lathrop, president of the American Fund for French Wounded.

bad since we have been here. No one pays any attention to the cannon and there has [*sic*] only been two air raids, neither of which amounted to much. I guess that the Allies have the supremacy of the air and are keeping the Germans too busy at the front to allow them enough time for raids on towns behind the lines. It must be that because if the Germans had the equipment I do not think that they would have stopped the raids. It is not like them. They succeeded in driving a million people out of Paris and I guess if they kept up the work they could scare out a few more. With the exception of a few beautiful days, the weather has been very cold and dark since we arrived and probably that accounts for the lack of raids as much as anything else. Over here, instead of looking at the sky on a clear night and saying "We're going to have a beautiful day tomorrow," people shake their heads and say "Well it's a fine night for a raid. I'll meet you later in the cellar." When the signal is heard everyone jumps into some clothes, grabs their passports and money and makes for the cave. You are never scared, no one is, but you have the feeling of expecting something—you don't know just what.

Then, when it is all over, all the church bells in Paris peal out the glad tiding and you almost feel that the war is over. Although my next letters may be written from "Somewhere in France" we will be free from raids and cannons. We do not know yet whether we can tell where we are when we get there but I think that we can. I see no reason in being secretive about the whereabouts of a canteen.

Well, must close now as the Madame is up in our room giving Dode a French lesson and my turn comes next. Write often as it seems great to hear from home or Florida or wherever you are.

Love to all,
Al

9 May 1918

Dear Mama, Dad and all—

I have been waiting for the last two days to write to you until I had something definite to tell you of our plans but things move so slowly in France that we have had a hard time getting things settled. The trouble was that the cars Lathrop expected months ago have not arrived yet and she kept telling us to wait just a little longer and she would hear from them and in the meanwhile we could do odd jobs to keep us busy. Well, we did odd jobs for a month but it was not a satisfactory plan because we felt all the time that we could do more good someplace else and every day would hear that they were searching the highways and byways for American girls to work with the Red Cross. We finally took things into our own hands and went to the Red Cross and asked them if they would take us on and they said that we were more valuable than gold and that they would take us in a minute if we could get a release from Mrs. Lathrop. She held off at first but we finally arranged things so now belong to the American Red Cross and wear a big U S on our shoulder and feel like real soldiers. The Red Cross said today that they could place fifty American girls before tomorrow noon if they had them and that the thing to do was to find out what department needs us the most. We have a meeting with them tomorrow morning and by tomorrow night will know just where they want to send us. I think it will be either in the canteen dept or the Home Communication Service that they are installing in the hospitals for the American Wounded who are too ill to write home and tell their families what has happened to them. Either work will be wonderfully interesting and we are just crazy to get started at it. The Red Cross is having a hard time getting all the people they need as the U S is using all ships for transports. We got over just in time. Had we waited a month longer we never could have made it. At least that is what they tell us over here.

You don't know how good it was to get your first letter written from New York and the one from Chicago followed it the next day. I hope you are getting all the letters I have written and also the cable I sent from Paris. Mrs. Kellogg[46] is going to wire you whenever she gets word from Dode—will you always wire her please? Did not receive the shoestrings yet but suppose they will be along before long. You were right about the packages—no Americans in France can receive things from America.

The typewriter tape has gone to the dogs—will write again tomorrow.

Love to all,
Alice

What I wanted to say was that it is very nice to have candy and all that, but we really don't need it. We have plenty—too much—good food—Enclosed find proof—some of my unused bread tickets.

Love again,
"Al"

⁓

11 May 1918

Dear Mama and All—

I have anxiously scanned the table every time I return to our little room, on the third floor back to see if it holds a letter from home but never any luck. We heard that a mail boat arrived two days ago and feel sure that it carried letters for us. We received a wonderful box of "Smiths," addressed to the Misses O'Brien, Davis, and Kellogg but

---

46. Doris Kellogg's parents, Spencer and Jane M. Kellogg, lived in Buffalo, New York.

with no card enclosed.[47] It was more than welcomed and we send a thousand thanks to our beneficent donator over seas, whomever He or She may be. As I lay on the bed reading the Saturday Evening Post and munching "Smiths," I almost felt as if I was back in old St. Paul.

We are all signed up with the Red Cross, they were delighted to get us, but we won't know for four days where our canteen will be. It takes us that long to get our out of town papers then we will get our orders. We feel very grand in our uniforms with the Red Cross and U. S. on our shoulders and were quite taken off our feet today when many of the soldiers we passed saluted us. We don't know whether to smile, bow or return the salute. We ordered our caps and aprons for the canteen work today so have nothing to do but sit and wait for orders. However, we have a fascinating place to wait in. I suppose Paris is the most interesting city in the world today and we run our legs off trying to see all we can before our sojourn to the country. We are crazy to get started and can hardly wait to see where they'll send us.

Continue to send my mail to Morgan-Harjes[48] and I will leave a forwarding address there. They are awfully nice and accurate about mail and things. There is another Alice O'Brien [sic][49] with the Red Cross Canteen—she is from Buffalo and Dode knows her—hope she won't get all my mail. She won't if you use the Morgan-Harjes address. All of her stuff goes direct to Red Cross.

---

47. "Smith's on Sixth" was a St. Paul candy shop at the corner of Sixth and Robert, owned by J. George Smith. The 1918 R. L. Polk City Directory described the store as "Maker Smith's Internationally Popular Chocolate Dreams and Smith's Delicious Counter Specials." Smith's had a shop in Minneapolis, too.

48. Morgan-Harjes was an investment bank with locations in Paris, London, New York, and Philadelphia. It eventually became J. P. Morgan & Company.

49. Alice Lord O'Brian was from Buffalo, New York. Her own letters were published under the title *No Glory: Letters from France 1917–1919*, by Airport Publishers of Buffalo, in 1936.

The Red Cross is wonderful and has done more than anything else to cement the feeling between France and America. They are running Hospitals, Ambulances, Canteens, Home Communications Service for Soldiers, Identification Bureau, Transports, Supply Service, Caring for Refugees, Consumptives, Mutilated Soldiers, Babies, the old and the young—helping anywhere where help is needed and that is a universal need over here. Major Olds says that they have not half as many people as they need and that in a month there is going to be three jobs for every American man or woman in France. No one talks of going home until the work is over and I guess that will be a long time from now.

We had dinner with Keith Clark last night. She is doing publicity work for the Y.W.C.A. Mrs. Forest has left Paris and is in the country doing some sort of research work among the soldiers.

We are going to the Olds again, to dinner, they have been so very nice to us. We see Mr. Bobbett now and then. He is in the Finance Department of the Red Cross and working hard.

If Jack is set on getting here why doesn't he apply with the Red Cross. There are lots of splendid men working with them who were disqualified as soldiers and there is loads of interesting work to be done. I should think he would rather do that than get in with the *Canadiens* and get sidetracked.

Tell Teta that I am keeping my eyes open for a job for her and that if she gets a cable to pack and come. I know she would enjoy the air raids.

Love to all—will write soon again
Alice

18 May 1918

Dear Mama and All—

At last—we have received our orders and are to go to the Red Cross canteen at Chantille [*sic*], a little town about forty minutes from Paris. We are to be with the French soldiers, that is to say, the canteen is called a French canteen although the troops are so mixed around that they get a lot of Americans coming thru the same canteens as the French. I am glad that we are to work first with the French because you can not [*sic*] be here without realizing how wonderful they have been for the last four years and you feel that you want to do all you can for them. The canteen is one of the large ones and is run by an American Woman, called a Directress, and under her about seventeen American Girls. Mrs. W. K. Vanderbilt[50] of New York is at the head of the canteen Dept. for the Red Cross and all our arrangements have been made with her. She is more than nice, works from nine every morning to six every night and is wrapt [*sic*] up in the success of the work. We have seen Lois Brundred[51] and she has finished her six months term and has just signed up for another three months. She says that canteen work is the most interesting work of the war and she would not change into any other branch for anything in the world. Be sure to get the "Saturday Evening Post" for April sixth and read the article in it by Elizabeth Frazer called "A Canteen in France." We read it the other day and that girl's experiences were so like our own, especially the part about leaving

---

50. Anne Harriman Sands Rutherfurd Vanderbilt and her husband, William K. Vanderbilt, were active supporters of the war efforts in France. Anne was a founder of the American Ambulance Corps at Neuilly.

51. Lois Brundred (1889–), from Pennsylvania, was one of the earlier Red Cross volunteers in France, arriving in September 1917.

America, that it thrilled us to read it. The article is written about the canteen at Issoudun[52] and all the pictures were taken there.

One other reason that I am glad to be with the French is that it will be so good for our French. Doris and I have been taking about two lessons a week and have picked up quite a bit but just enough to teach me how little I really know so I will be glad to have the opportunity to use a little of it.

We have hied ourselves to the cellar for the past two nights at the sound of the alert but both times have been false alarms. I wonder what the American papers say about the air raids? They amount to so little that people hardly mention them here but I suppose they feature them with headlines in the Pioneer Press. We are getting mail quite regularly now and it is nice to hear from home. I received the clipping that you sent me about the Liberty Loan campaign and am immensely proud of Dad's subscription. That's the way to lick the Kaiser. Received Auntie Marie's letter and she intimated that the Burton Schwartz deal was on.[53] Isn't that fine. I hope that it will go thru all right. She also said that you and Dad had hied yourselves off [to] the French Lick.[54] Aren't you the gay sports though? And Robert[55] is sixteen? I wrote him a birthday letter do hope he received it.

You don't know how sick we all were when we found that you had not received your cables. We arrived on the tenth day and all said that you would receive cables before you really started worrying and you don't know [how] disappointed we are about them. Dode,

---

52. Issoudun, a commune in the Indre department in central France, was the location of the largest training center for the US Air Service, with more than ten thousand people stationed there.

53. Burton-Schwartz was a lumber and railroad company located in Florida. Alice's father, William, partnered with its owners on some efforts there.

54. The French Lick Hotel in Indiana was a popular spa and golf resort. Its owners claim credit for first serving tomato juice in 1917, the same year Alice's parents visited. www.frenchlick.com.

55. Alice's brother Robert O'Brien.

Mugs and Genevieve all cabled from the boat at Bordeaux and I waited, because I was sure you would hear thru Mrs. Kellogg also the Davises,[56] until we got to Paris and then I sent one. I can not understand how they all went wrong. We have started an investigation and may get our money back but even that is far from satisfactory. It is very difficult to cable from this side but there is no trouble about getting cables from America. If you ever cable me send it to Morgan-Harjes and they will wire it to me wherever I am. If I feel flush I will send you one now and then.

You don't know how beautiful Paris is at this time of the year. I so often think when I see interesting things that we all must come over after the war and see all the wonderful things that are here. When I look at Notre Dame and think that the Germans have destroyed Rheims it just seems too wicked. If they ever get to Paris they will raze it to the ground it has withstood them so long. Every one is anxiously waiting for the much talked of resumption of the big offensive. The papers are full of the plans that the Germans are making and all wonder at what part of the line they are going to make their big strike. They say that they are getting ready for the biggest push of all but that the Allies are prepared to receive them and that their spirit is as unquenchable as ever. Isn't it wonderful after all they have gone thru? You don't hear people here ever hoping for Peace, nothing but a smashing Victory is going to satisfy them even if it takes years to win it.

The Red Cross is busy getting our papers to allow us to work at Chantilly and in the meanwhile asked us to stop in and help out in the casualty department so we work in the office every day from nine to twelve and again from two to six. It is very interesting work but very sad to enlist all the names of the wounded and killed soldiers

---

56. Marguerite Davis's parents, Herbert and Jennie Davis, lived in St. Paul.

and all the particulars concerning the casualties. The dept also locates soldiers whose families have not heard from them for months and the number of such cases is surprising. I read many letters today from men and women in America who had been trying to locate their sons, brothers, etc., whom they have not heard from since their arrival in France but saddest of all are the letters written by the Home Communication Bureau to the families in America whose sons have been killed in battle. The searcher always writes a personal letter, telling where the soldier is buried, how he was killed, who saw him last, how bravely he fought and so on. When you think of all the homes in America that are going to receive such letters before this hideous war is over it makes you realize how ghastly it is. All the military authorities are crazy about the fine spirit of the American Boys and the way they fight. They are making wonderful aviators but are still flying French planes. Something seems to have gone awfully wrong with the American airplane construction. Every week sees fifty thousand more kaki [sic] clad men arrive in France and each one of them only wanting to raise the devil with the Huns. Well, everyone wishes them well, they are the heroes of the day and won't it be a wonderful day when they return to America victorious?

Doris says that it is time to go to bed. We have worked hard today and feel like the old village blacksmith, "Something accomplished, something done, has earned a night's repose" and if the damned Germans come tonight and disturb our peaceful slumber I'll start for Berlin in the morning.

Am enclosing a picture so you can see our uniform. I can just hear you saying that I look as pale as a sheet but I assure you that it is a bad picture and that I have never felt better in my life. Everyone here has and expects to have a constant cold but I have not even so much as sneezed since I struck the place. Now what have you got to say about my bad throat? Dr. Carmen didn't quite ruin it after all.

Dode and I are going to Notre Dame in the morning and then walk around the neighborhood and pick out all the old spots. The most beautiful church in Paris is right here, the Sainte Chapelle. It is a lovely little Gothic chapel that was built in the time of St. Louis and is the most beautiful thing I have ever seen.

Good night, I hope you sleep as well as I do.
Love,
Alice

~

28 May 1918
[Metropolitan Hotel, Paris]

Dear Mama, Dad and all—

Yesterday was a big day for me because when I got to the bank the mail clerk handed me four letters, two from Mama, one from Jack and one from Aunt Lorene but I am still waiting for Auntie Marie's first. Isn't it nice that she is going to New York. She will have a good time, a change of interest and will get back to St. Paul full of pep for the Red Cross. And Hurray for Jack! I hope his engine will continue to run as merrily until all the logs are out. Make a lot of cash Jack because after the war we are going to have a "Grande tour de l'Europe, en famille, dans motor." I plan it every day. And I will lead personally conducted parties all over Paris pointing to the shots that Big Bertha struck.

The offensive is on again and everyone in Paris is praying for the Allied Armies. Poor brave fellows, I suppose hundreds of them are dying on the battlefields only sixty miles away. The Huns recommenced with all their fury and this time, hope to gain all that they expected to during their offensive of March. Everyone knows that they won't but it is going to take time to down them. At half past six yesterday morning we heard the big gun roar so we knew the offensive was on because the cannon has not been heard in Paris for twenty days. They continued to drop a shell every twenty minutes for about three hours and then let up till late in the afternoon when they commenced again.[57] About eleven last night the sirens shrieked their warning and everyone waited for the Gothas to arrive but they were turned back north of the city so soon after the "all clear" was given and everyone went peacefully to sleep. This morning Bertha started again at daylight and has popped three or four times during the forenoon. The Germans are obviously (the cannon just boomed again! Away off in the distance, sounding like a sunset gun at Fort Snelling) trying to break down the moral [sic] of France by scaring the civil population so badly that industry will suffer from it but they have a long way to go.[58] No one pays any attention to their silly old cannon and every air raid makes people resolve to see this war won if it takes years to do it. The Germans are just like animals, haven't the spirit or courage of humanity, and they think just because the fat slobs in Cologne get excited about the last British Raid that the French people are going to get scared to death of them and yell for Peace. I wish the Allied Air Force would blow every town in Germany to pieces. I wish I had a little aeroplane of my own to use on these bright, sun-shiny afternoons.

Dode, Mugs and I were walking along the Place de la Concorde yesterday morning on our way to the Red Cross, talking excitedly about the offensive, when the Big Gun landed a shell a few blocks away with a bang that must have been heard in New York. Mugs gave one whoop and went three feet into the air. An old Frenchman was passing, many in fact, but this one in particular threw back his

---

57. May 27, the start of the third effort, "Blücher-Yorck," in the Spring Offensive began with a similarly blistering bombardment on the area between Soissons and Reims. This time, the guns met with particularly weak resistance, and the Germans broke through. By the end of the day, the Germans had made the longest single-day advance since the trench warfare had begun. Cruttwell, *History of the Great War*, 526.

58. The Germans advanced to within thirty-seven miles of Paris that day, and the bombs were not just for show. The citizens of Paris were justifiably frightened, and many fled the city. Cruttwell, *History of the Great War*, 527.

head and roared. I think it was the first good laugh he had since the war started and he went down the street doubled over with mirth.

We moved yesterday and are now at the Metropolitan Hotel. We lived so far from the Red Cross that it was difficult for us to get there at nine every morning and a long way to go back at night when we were tired. We have stored our trunks at the Y.W.C.A. hotel for the summer because we are going to travel light when we start for the canteen. Only our uniforms and work aprons, waists and underwear are necessary. We have been working hard in the casualty department but are crazy to get started on our own job because it is hard to settle down into a thing when you know it is only temporary. I think that the canteen will seem quite tame after the air raids and the bombarding of Paris but I guess we will have enough to keep us busy without looking for excitement. The soldiers say that there are two fronts in France now, Paris and the trenches.

No, I have not seen Andrew,[59] in fact I have not even got his address or his regiment number but wish you would get it from Minnie Comstock and send it to me. I wish I had it now because I could tell from the casualty lists whether or not his regiment was in the line. I have not seen the Birminghams, don't think I would know them if I did but perhaps they would know me. Heard from Al Warren and wrote to him but I do not think we will see him soon as he is in an Artillery School and can not get to Paris and I am afraid that when he does get here we will be off in a canteen. If you meet people over here you just happen to run into them, you can never plan it.

We will be in the country and far from the maddening sound of bombs by the time you receive this letter so do not worry about me any more when you read in the Pioneer Press all about the Paris raids. And, by the way, always send my mail to Morgan-Harjes, Blvd. Haussmann. There are so many people in the Red Cross, just think

---

59. Likely Andrew DeGraff Berkey (1888–1967), a friend from St. Paul.

of it there are several thousand Americans here with the Red Cross alone, that the mail addressed there is apt to get messed up so I will keep Morgan-Harjes for my permanent address. My letter of credit is O.K. no trouble at all about it. If I need the money in the Bank at home I will write to you to forward it to me. I feel quite rich when I think of my dividends over there accumulating.

Washburn's car is not here yet or the one from Coleraine. There are all sorts of rumours running around about the motor service of the A.F.F.W. and I guess we are lucky to be out of it. We struck it at a bad time, everything is in a mess and it will take sometime to straighten out. Some of the trouble is due to the A.F.F.W. management and some of it to the ordinary exigencies of war. We are glad to be wearing the Red Cross. It represents so much over here and everything is so businesslike about it. Many of the finest men and women in America are in France volunteering their time and money and working over time and they are a fine crowd to work with. They need several hundred more American girls and are rather worried about getting them here because it is getting to be more and more difficult. Lots of them arrive on every boat but they soon disappear into the melting pot, get into uniform and start work. When you see a girl in ordinary clothes you always know that she has just arrived.

Love to you all—We are just starting back to the Red Cross for the afternoon. Can hardly wait for the evening papers to see how the line is holding.[60]

Love again,
Alice

~

---

60. The line was not holding very well. The Allied troops continued to buckle, and were unable to hold the line until June 2. Cruttwell, *History of the Great War*, 527.

3 June 1918
Paris

Dear Mama, Dad and all—

I have been trying for fifteen minutes to think, not what to write about, but what not to write about. So many things unexpected happen over here and so suddenly, that it is hard to keep you posted as to just what is going on. Before I start this letter proper I want to say, lest I forget, that I received your letter saying that you had sent Dick a check for the typewriter. I am so glad that that little affair is settled and that we can forget about it as we were wondering how in the world we were going to get word to him.

We were working in the casualty dept, waiting for our papers for Chantilly, when the offensive started and simultaneously the American attack on Chatigny [Cantigny].[61] The wounded started to pour into Paris and in twenty four hours the hospitals were crowded to the doors, beds in all corridors, operations going on all day and night, men's wounds being dressed in wards, hallways or wherever they could get room to lay them, the nurses and Doctors so busy that the half well patients had to wait on the others, in fact everything in pell mell shape and all organization swept off its feet by the rush. We were sent out to Hospital No. 1, used to be the American Ambulance, at Neuilly, just outside of Paris and only fifteen minutes from Place de la Concorde, and told to do whatever we could to help. Girls are being taken from all sorts of work and put into hospitals to help out during the present emergency. Few of them have had any hospital experience, you can imagine how much I know about such things, but we soon learn.

---

61. The first battle on the Western Front for American troops was at Cantigny on May 28. The Americans successfully retook the village and helped build confidence for themselves and all the Allies.

Hospital No. 1 is a huge place, with twelve hundred beds, and when I saw it, filled to the overflow with American and French wounded, I wondered that there were any men left at the front to check the Germans. The first morning we reported we were put into a bed-making squad and, I swear, I think we made every one of the twelve hundred beds. In the afternoon we did what we could for the soldiers in the corridors, getting them water, putting cloths on their heads, fixing their pillows and cheering them up. So many of them have been gassed and I feel almost sorrier for them than I do for the ones that are suffering from gun shot wounds, shrapnel or otherwise. The gas very often burns their bodies horribly but always affects their eyes, throats and lungs. It is unspeakably sad to see the poor fellows doubled over in an agony of coughing and realize what they must be suffering. It is hard enough to cough with a healthy throat but think what it must be when the entire back of it has been burned out with mustard gas. There is very little to do for gas patients, they just have to lie and wait for time to cure them if they ever are cured. Most of them lose their voices, temporarily, and the ones that can talk speak in a low, sepulchral tone as though they were speaking from the grave. Many of them suffer from lack of nourishment because their throats are so sore that they cannot eat.

The next day we made beds, assisted with the general work in the wards, gave the men their meals, medicines, took temperatures, pulses, wrote out reports, took the dressings from the wounds and got the patients ready for the Doctor, and listened to the tales of the trenches told by wounded soldiers who, twenty four hours before, had been crawling on their hands and knees through no mans land, shells whistling over them, men dropping on all sides, battle planes circling over their heads and they wondering whether they were going to be able to drag themselves to the dressing station or were destined to sink into a shell hole and die. It is almost like being in the trenches to talk to those men, still covered with mud, their

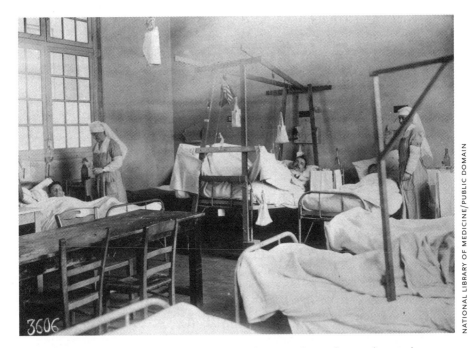

Crowded conditions and pragmatic medical care at the Red Cross hospital at Neuilly.

clothes shot full of holes, faces haggard, eyes swollen and burnt, and their bloody dressings, put on in a field hospital, a constant reminder of the hell they have just come thru. And the wonderful part of it all is that they are aching to get back and have another swipe at the Fritzies. We have heard some harrowing tales of hand to hand fighting, treatment of prisoners, and taking of dugouts but I will have to wait until I see you to tell you of them. If I started I would write all night and I can't do that as we have to be up and away early in the morning.

Today was our fifth as auxiliary nurses and I can not believe that we have done all that we really have. The Nurse on my corridor has charge of four wards and has an auxiliary nurse in charge of each ward, all under her orders but enough responsibility, at that, to make my knees shake under me. I am the auxiliary in ward 237, the nurse comes in three or four times a day, but the rest of the time I am left alone to sink or swim with ten French blesses,[62] one Russian and four Americans whose beds are in the corridor right outside the door. If you would like to know a few of the things I did today, read the following—Washed faces and hands, made beds for the ones not seriously ill—gave Dakin treatment to men whose wounds were being treated with it—removed dressings from all wounds so that they would be ready for the Doctor (some of the wounds are dreadful and some not so bad, the Russian has had his leg amputated just below the knee, one man has dreadful head wounds, one has a shrapnel wound the size of a saucer in the middle of his back, one has the calf of his leg shot away, one, a poor young French boy, has a bayonet wound thru the abdomen and I am afraid that he is mortally ill, and one has a gun shot wound that enters one side of his body and comes out the other. Most of these men get the Dakin treatment, a system of drains and wet bandages). Assisted the nurse and Doctor at the dressings—bound up all wounds after dressings—made the Russian's bed, a slow and painful operation—took all pulses and temperatures—gave them their luncheon—did Lord knows what all afternoon—gave them dinner and at six came home to my own, tired as a dog but thoroughly satisfied and happy with the days [sic] work. I would have to have training and experience, in America, before I would be allowed to do half of what I did today but, over here, they tell you to do the best you can and you go ahead knowing that if you didn't do them no one else would, and I suppose, something is better than nothing. I am sorry that the men in my ward are not lucky enough to have an A number one nurse but I give them the best I have and pray for results.

Must retire now—will add to this tomorrow—

---

62. French for "wounded men."

The following night

Never, never, have I been so elated. We just heard that the Allies have captured fifty thousand prisoners. It was officially announced at the hospital today and everyone is speechless with joy. We will be a sick crowd tomorrow if we learn that the information was not reliable but for the present, at least, we tread on air. Isn't it wonderful! It is almost too good to be true. If it is correct Paris will be the happiest place in the world tomorrow.

I am getting along wonderfully well with my ward. All ten Frenchmen and the Russian were as happy as clams today and just as comfortable as they could expect to be considering the wounds they have. They suffer terribly while their wounds are being dressed but seem to be very happy as soon as the Doctor leaves, I guess it is a treat for most of them just to lay quietly in bed, far away from the whistling of shells and flying shrapnel. They all smile broad smiles when I appear in the morning and one by one, in the most polite manner, say "Good morning, Nees." When I go out to luncheon they wish me a good appetite and when I leave for the night they wish me a pleasant sleep. They are so pleased and grateful over any little thing that you do for them that it is a pleasure to do it. The manners of a French *Poilu*[63] are enough to put those of a good American private to shame.

The rush at No. 1 still continues, some of the Doctors operated all last night and the day shift started at five this morning. I suppose things will be worse than ever for the next week or so because we hear that an American contingent has been put into the offensive at its hottest point.

The past week has been an anxious one for France. The German advance was quite depressing but it seems to be stemmed at present. Loads of people have left Paris but the ones doing war work never

---

63. *Poilu* was the informal term for the French infantrymen.

think of such a thing. Everything sinks into insignificance except the work you are doing and the harder you work the happier you are. We have been having air raids every night, sometimes two a night, but the barrage is so good that the Gothas seldom break thru. Of course, when the guns begin to roar you never know whether you are listening to defense guns or exploding bombs so that makes things rather exciting at times. It is not until you read the next morning's paper that you know just what happened, how many German planes over Paris, how many bombs dropped, how many wounded, etc, etc. The long distance cannon has been booming away daily but the population has learned to take it for granted and it does not cause half the commotion that the three meatless days a week stirred up. The French do hate food restrictions.

I think I will draw this long letter to a close. Don't worry about me. I am well, safe and HAPPY. I think I waste more time thinking about you worrying about me than you do worrying about me, perhaps. But I do hope that you don't spend sleepless nights or get horrible qualms when you read the sensational news in the morning papers. Take everything with a grain of salt—things are a lot better over here than they look in America. I am not the one to worry about. It is quite the other way about because I am only sorry that you all are over there and missing out on the things that are going on over here.

Hope you all are well. Have not heard from you for ten days but an American ship is due tomorrow and I expect mail the next day. Love to all of you. Why not show this letter to the Bends?[64] I intend to write them soon but am so busy now that it is about all I can do to take a hot bath and crawl into bed.

Love to all,
Alice

---

64. Mr. and Mrs. Harold P. Bend.

Next a.m.

My hopes are dashed—no news in the morning paper about the 50,000—[65]

∿

8 June 1918

Dear Mama, Dad and All—

Tomorrow will be our last day at the Hospital as we have received our papers and orders to leave for Chantilly on Monday morning. We hate to leave the hospital because we have been gripped by the interest of the work but I am sure that we will be just as enthusiastic about the canteen when we get there. We are truly under military orders now, ordered here and there just like the soldiers in the army, and it is great to be a part of such a huge, efficient organization. You spoke in your last letter about my time being up—it looks to me as though the Americans that were over here are due to stick and see things out, regardless of what private plans they may have made. No one talks about going home and most people are signed up for duration of war. We do as we're told to do, over here, that is we do since we have joined a real organization. The Canteen Dept. is under the bureau of Military affairs and we are subject to army orders just as much as any low private.

---

65. Though the report of fifty thousand German prisoners of war was inaccurate, it was not the number but the nationality of the soldiers that was wrong. Shockingly, the Germans had captured just over fifty thousand *Allied* soldiers by May 30 during this effort. A total of seventy thousand Allied prisoners of war were captured by the Germans by June 13. Cruttwell, *History of the Great War,* 528.

Our hospital experience has been wonderful, if we stay here long enough we will have a swing at every kind of war work. I can not write about lots of things that I have seen and heard from the soldiers and I can just see Teta falling in a faint when I get back home and start telling you about them. Dad always says that there is nothing in the world that human nature won't get used to and it has never seemed truer to me than in the past week. I see and do things that would raise the hair off my head if I were reading about them but nowadays I take them just as calmly as I take the rest of life. I had to hold a man down in bed yesterday, leaning my full weight on his chest and holding his hands down, while his wounds were being dressed. It took about ten minutes and during the entire dressing he shrieked with pain, prayed out loud for relief and called for his Mother. Some of the men are in wonderful condition and can stand all sorts of things but others are suffering from shell and nerve shock and they cry like children. Poor kids, I can't say enough for them. America will win the war but it will be at their expense and a lot of them won't be alive to enjoy the day of victory. The Red Cross is truly marvelous. They are saving thousands of lives and I hate to think of the terrible things that would go on if the Red Cross were not here to do their part. Everything that the army can not do they turn over to the Red Cross and it has never failed yet. When you think that the people of America have donated millions of dollars for the comfort of others it speaks pretty well for the country. But if they could see how much good their money does and how badly it is needed they would double the amount.

Every American in Paris is wildly excited about the way the American boys are fighting. They are wonderful and I wish you could read what the French papers say about them, they can't say enough. France and England have been anxiously waiting for their first real trial because the Amex Forces, as they call them here, exceeded all hopes in their last two splendid attacks, at Cantigny and at Chateau-Thierry.[66] There are forty doctors, one hundred nurses and eighty-five nurses aides at No. 1 but they were not able to take care of the wounded as fast as they arrived after the attack at Chateau-Thierry. Seven Hundred came in on one day and each one of them had to be registered, undressed, put to bed, his wounds dressed, washed and given three meals a day. Most of them had to go to the operating room to be x-rayed and then operated on to remove the shrapnel—can you imagine the confusion and the unspeakable suffering? We did not get home until half past eight last night and we started out again this morning at eight. The work is never done but goes on unendingly from shift to shift. They operate day and night but are never finished.

The big gun goes off occasionally but we are too busy to even hear it. When you are in the hospital it is like living in another world and when we get back to the hotel it is like going from hades into heaven. We lose an hour or so of sleep now and then on account of the air raids, they make a dreadful racket but apparently seem to do little damage. The refugees have been pouring through Paris by the thousands for the past few days, some of them come by boat and some by train. The girls [who] have been working at the stations say that they are a pitiful lot, thrown out on the world with nothing except what is on their backs. But the Red Cross comes to the rescue again, feeds them, gives them clothing and a place to sleep for the night and the next day sends them down to southern France where they can work on farms, or if they are not able to work, live in one of the many refugee camps.

---

66. In late May, the Americans were helping to defend the area near Château-Thierry against the third effort of the Spring Offensive. When Château-Thierry fell to the Germans on June 1, the battle shifted to the nearby Belleau Wood. American troops fought to hold the Germans and began a counterattack on June 6. The Battle of Belleau Wood continued through to June 26. Grant, *World War I: The Definitive Visual History,* 284.

I will not write again from Paris as we leave the day after tomorrow but will write you a full description of our new station and job. We are going to be with twenty other American girls and a Mrs. Church,[67] who is the directress. Every one says that she is one of the nicest directresses over here so I think we are lucky to be under her. We are going to the Olds for a farewell supper tomorrow night, we will stop there on our way from the hospital. Mrs. Olds says that it is to be a very special party and we are going to have pancakes and maple syrup. I never eat the dirty things in America but they are such a treat over here that I will have to eat them if they kill me.

Well, this is bath night, you can only have hot water twice a week in France, Saturday and Sunday, so I must have a tub and turn in. Was glad to hear more about the cypress deal—tell me all about it—payments, etc.[68] Dode and I have had summer uniforms made, grey mohair and they are very jaunty. I shall hate to get out of uniform and back into regular clothes when I get home because they are so comfortable.

Love to you all—write often as I love to get your letters. You were a sport to march in the parade. I expect to see you in France before long. Ask Teta if she wants me to find her a job over here. Really I wish she would come over because there is lots she could do. Why doesn't Jack come over with the Red Cross if he wants to. There are loads of men working with them who have been refused by the army.

Love,
Al

~

---

67. Likely Margaret Philip Church (1883–), a graduate of Lee Private Hospital in Rochester, New York.

68. Likely the Burton-Schwartz agreement that Alice refers to in other letters.

14 June 1918
"Somewhere in France" [Chantilly]

Dear Mama and Dad and all—

Notice the heading—I am acting according to orders but you know where I am as I wrote it to you some time ago from Paris. We have been here for several days but I have been too busy to find time to write you before. ——is in the French war zone but don't let that frighten you because everything outside of Paris is in the zone these days.[69] As a matter of fact, Paris is the most warlike place we have struck and coming here is like going to the country for a rest as we have only an occasional air raid and have no such unpleasant thing as the long range cannon to bother us. It is a wonderful opportunity to be here and to see all the sights we see. Of course all our mail goes thru the military censor now so I have to be even more careful than before if I want all the letters to get thru. Lots of the girls have had letters lost in the censor bureau because they were rather indiscreet about what they wrote but it is awfully hard to know what you can write and what you must leave out. If possible I will have this mailed in Paris and it will leave sooner.

First I will tell you about the canteen. We live in——, in a darling little house that is owned by some English people but is now rented to the Red Cross and all the canteen workers at this post live in it. It is as attractive as it can be, furnished with beautiful old stuff, gay French wall papers, a winding staircase, a sweet garden, old fashioned shutters and is called the White House. The canteen is at——

---

69. This was pretty much true. The fourth and final German effort of the Spring Offensive, called Gneisenau by the Germans and known as the Noyon-Montdidier Offensive, had just occurred June 9–12 along the Matz River, north of Compiègne. The Germans had sought to connect their two salients and initially succeeded, but a French counterattack on June 11 stopped their momentum.

[Orry-la-Ville], about three miles away and we go back and forth by train usually but sometimes by the canteen camion. The personnel consists of Mrs. Church, the directress, fifteen American girls all volunteers like ourselves, one chaufeur [*sic*] and about fifteen servants (cooks, dishwashers, vegetable parers, scrubwomen, etc). The canteen is open day and night but the big rush comes for dinner at noon and for supper at five-thirty. The first shift of workers goes on at seven-fifteen in the morning and comes off at two-thirty in the afternoon. The second shift overlaps the first and comes on at twelve, noon, and goes off at seven-thirty in the evening and the night shift comes on at seven and goes off at seven. The night shift does not work all thru the night but only at train hours. There is a room next to the canteen where the night shift can snatch some sleep when they are not busy and then, as they get the whole next day off, they have plenty of time to rest, in fact it is the easiest shift of all. Mugs has been on the first shift since we arrived and Dode and I have been on the second. We have an early lunch down in the cunning little dining room, tear off to the canteen and return in time for a late dinner with all the rest of the girls, usually about eight-thirty. The hours do not sound long, in fact, when I first arrived I was rather disappointed because I was afraid that we were not needed for a full days work, but if you could see the pace we go while on duty, you would think that seven or eight hours was plenty for one day. We feed about a thousand men each noon and about the same each evening. The number for breakfast always varies. In addition to the main canteen, where regular full size meals are served, we operate a place called "La goute," which means "The Drop," and is a little booth where the Poilus[70]

---

70. The French word *Poilu* means "hairy one," and was a term of endearment used to describe the French infantrymen in World War I. The reference was likely inspired by the moustaches and beards that were popular among the men, who were often from agricultural backgrounds.

can get hot coffee or chocolate, sandwiches and hard-boiled eggs at any time of day. The French govt. will not allow the Red Cross to give things to the Poilus free of charge because they say that it is a bad thing to get them into the habit of expecting it so the R.C. is obliged to charge them a little but of course, gives them far more than they pay for. For instance, they pay two cents for coffee, four cents for chocolate and fifteen cents for a full meal consisting of good meat, potatoes, a vegetable, salad which by the way they cannot live without, a bowl of soup, a hunk of bread, dessert which is usually fruit or nuts and raisins or stewed fruit, and a cigarette. The poor souls are delighted with what they get and you would die to hear them thank the management and the extravagant praise that they tender to the Red Cross should be handed down to posterity. When they all pile into the refrectory [sic] it looks as tho a blue cloud had taken possesion [sic] of the place and the other day as I watched them I could hardly keep the tears back. They are so sad, have been fighting for four years, are pitifully poor and most of them leave huge families behind when they go off to the trenches. You see the canteen is at a station called a "station for *permission-aires.*" All the soldiers whose permission of leave are over (each man gets ten days every six months) come to——and there receives orders where to join his regiment, at what part of the front, etc. Many of them get their last good meal before they enter the trenches, and unhappily, many of them have their last real meal on earth in our canteen. We have a phonograph which plays while they eat and most of them are the happiest crowd in the world, they laugh and sing and always have a pleasant word for everyone and twenty minutes after they shoulder their packs, gas masks, shovels, rifles, blanket rolls, canteen, mount the train and are off to the trenches. Their spirit is wonderful and the Germans are barking up the wrong tree when they think that cannon and shells can destroy the morale of France.

The "White House" where Alice, Marguerite Davis, and Doris Kellogg stayed in Chantilly. An American flag flies from the second-story window.

Alice serving coffee to soldiers at the "Gout de Café" at the canteen in Orry-la-Ville.

The first night here we stayed at the hotel, as our room at the White House was not ready for us, and our window opened onto the main square of this quaint, little town. The place is full of military activity and all night long, on the cobble stoned street outside our window we heard camions, horses, ambulances and troops of cavalry go past in a never ending stream. At about daybreak we were awakened by an unfamiliar shuffeling [sic] sound and looking out the window, we saw a regiment of blue coated Poilus march past towards the front. Their faded blue uniforms blended into the dawn as they marched farther and farther away and finally the scuffle of feet grew faint, the rumble of their voices ceased and it seemed as tho we were singularly alone. Almost as much as the one lone airplane patrolling the morning sky.

Yesterday afternoon, in front of the canteen, we saw the Poilus craning their necks to look at the sky so rushed out to see the excitement and were just in time to see an escradille of forty French planes go sailing over our heads like a flock of wild geese. It was a wonderful sight and it thrilled your imagination to know that they were off to battle over the enemy lines. I wonder how many returned. The French and English air service is wonderful—far better than the German—the Aviators seem like some sort of superhuman birds—they are wonderful.

Well—have been called to lunch so must eat in a rush and be off to work. We love being here—are under military orders and the protection of the Red Cross—are perfectly safe—the Red Cross always takes care of its personel [sic]—don't worry about me.

Will write soon again—Love to all
in a hurry,
Al

16 June 1918
[Canteen, Orry-la-Ville]

Dear Mama, Dad and all—

I hate to start to write a letter because I think of so many things that I cannot say. I will never get over how lucky we are to be here, right in the midst of things. Lots of girls have been here for over a year but have not seen half the things we have. I saw my first gang of German prisoners yesterday afternoon. One hundred and thirty-eight of them being marched straight from the front to a prison camp not far from here. They were rather an ungainly looking crowd of stiffs, horrid uniforms and stupid faces. Two German officers were among the rest, marched at the head of the column in a very dignified fashion, heads high and eyes straight ahead. It must have bit into them to be marching under the guns of the French Poilus. I would have loved to have taken a punch at one of the slobs but managed to restrain myself.

I am on the night shift at the canteen now. Go on at six in the evening, work till about half past twelve or one according to the size of the crowd we serve, sleep till five-thirty a.m., serve hot chocolate and coffee until seven-thirty when the day shift arrives and then take the train home. I spend most of the day in bed but usually get up about three o'clock when Dode comes off duty and then we take a walk about the town to see the sights, there is always something new as things change here every day, or else we walk over to the French field hospital which is only about two blocks off. It is a huge movable tent affair, very interesting to see but also very depressing because they have all the Grande Blesses (badly wounded) of the sector. Poor boys, it is terrible to see them suffer so and quite pathetic to see their faces light up with pleasure when we bring them little presents, cigarettes, oranges, *confiture* or whatever we are able to buy. I used to love to bring the American wounded cigarettes, in the hospital at

Neuilly, and thought that they needed them badly but when I see how little that the poor French have the Americans seem pampered. It isn't right—they all should have whatever they need or want—but I suppose that the war is so big and hard to manage that lots of little things slip past unheeded. The nurse in one of the wards was delighted when she saw us coming with oranges because she said the one of her patients was dying and had asked for an orange that morning but that she didn't have one to give him. He was so grateful when Dode put three beside his bed, the ghost of a smile flitted across his face, pale as the pillow it lay on, and then he closed his eyes as tho even that little smile had tired him. Your hearts would ache if you could see them, each so infinitely sad in himself and yet so small a part of the horror of the war. And yet it still goes on, the Germans are fighting with the bit between their teeth this summer and every one seems to think that it is their last great effort. They can never win, "They shall not pass" is the motto of the French army and the civilian population backs them up in every letter of it. They would have to kill every man, woman and child in France and they can't do that. They are not supernatural and they will go down sooner or later, with all the world against them. "Made in Germany" will never again be a trademark that is known around the world, they will have to disguise the fact if they ever want to sell their goods to civilized people.

I will try and draw you a plan of the canteen. I wish you could drop in some day at noon or at midnight and see the hundreds of French Poilus being fed. We have six fifteen gallon *marmites* on special stoves, steaming away all the time, filled with chocolate, coffee and bouillon. I have never seen so much coffee consumed in my life, they drink it by the quart and yell for more. Each man comes up to the counter with his ticket and gets his tray, all attractively arranged and looking very appetizing, and takes it back to one of the tables in the long hall. There they sit, hundreds of blue-coated figures, eating, laughing, talking or beating time to the funny, tinny phonograph that plays on unceasingly. Oh that phonograph,—we play it all the time because it means so much to them—but if I ever hated a thing in my life I hate that machine. We all pray that it will go wrong some day and will have to be sent to Paris for repairs. It will be a happy time for us. We all yell "Good luck" to the Poilus as they go off and then wonder how many of them will have it and how many of them will be buried "Somewhere."

I have not had a letter for over two weeks so expect several on the next mail. I don't care about the St. Paul papers but I would like it immensely if you would send me the New Republic now and then or the Literary Digest. I like to know what America thinks of what is going on and those are the two best editorial papers published. Did you read "Paris Under Fire" in one of the recent numbers of the New Republic? It was very interesting and true to life. If you keep in touch with those two papers you will know a lot more about what is going on over here than I can write you.

Well, going to have lunch now and sleep for a couple of hours.

Love to you all,
Alice
We are all well—

~

21 June 1918
[Canteen, Orry-la-Ville]

Dear Family—

I was just sick today when I got your letter and you said that you had not heard from me for twenty five days. I cannot understand it all

PLAN OF CANTINE

Rest Room *our*

Staff Rooms

Coffe Booth

KITCHEN

Photograph

Counter

counter

TABLES

This room holds over 1000 men

The room *holds*

Everything covered with French & American Flags

Alice's sketch of the canteen at Orry-la-Ville showed "this room holds over 1000 men."

because I have written at least twice a week and did not think I said anything that would be censored. Many of the girls say that they have had trouble in getting their letters across and I believe that the mails are very irregular but did not think that they were that bad. But, speaking of letters, there is nothing the matter with the mails coming in this direction because the letter I received today was written only three weeks ago but it was the first one I have received for three weeks. I was so disappointed when the mail from the last two boats had time to come but nothing on it for me. I know you are busy but if you have not time to write a long letter just say that you are well and let it go at that. You must have my letters by this time but in case you have not received them I will repeat—always send my mail or cablegrams to Morgan-Harjes. They will forward everything.

I note what you said about Max coming to France it does not worry or interest me much.[71] He is far from here now and even if he does get to the place he will find that it is very difficult to move around so I guess he won't bother us much. I think that Jack could come over with the Red Cross and do it on a lot less than three thousand dollars. I do not see how it could possibly take that much. Of course, you can spend all you have and more if you want to do it and the less French you know the more it costs you to live but most people over here live very simply and give what they can save to the people that you see every day and that are pitifully in need of it. Of course, as a rule it costs a man more to live than a girl but I don't know whether that would apply to war times or not. If Jack wants to come and can not find out enough about it over there I might be able to get a lot of information from Major Olds, find out just what he could do and all about it.

---

71. It is tempting to infer that Max may be a suitor, but no other evidence helps to explain this reference.

I am at the canteen, out in the coffee booth, and the place is surrounded by French soldiers and one lonesome Russian from the Foreign Legion. I am on night duty now but my week is almost finished and then I will work days again. We get about three or sometimes four hours sleep a night and then up in the morning at five or five-thirty, depends on the crowd. We serve breakfasts from the Goute and it is very picturesque in the early grey dawn to see the blue coated soldiers appear out of the misty woods. The Canteen is on the edge of a huge forest and on warm nights the soldiers sleep there instead of in the shelters made for them. We are on narrow strip of rightaway [*sic*] between the forest and the railroad track and the camp stretches along the track to the left of us. I bought a crayon sketch from a Poilu who was studying art before he was called to war so will be able to show you just how the place looks when I get there . . . Well, must close and get ready for our rushed hours. If this letter seems jerky it is because it has been interrupted so many times. The Poilus keep calling for coffee and chocolate and between times I punch a few keys. Love to all and I do hope that you have mail by now—Wish that the bunch of you would get together and manage to write me as many between you as I write home.

Love,
Al.

~

26 June 1918
[Chantilly]

Dear Mama, Dad and All—

Another letter from you today and still you say that you have not heard from me. I cannot believe it. This last letter was dated June sixth and you said that you had not heard from me for over four weeks. Something is wrong somewhere because I have written at least twice a week. This is my seventeenth letter to you, I have written twice to Auntie Marie, twice to Jack, once to Dad in Jacksonville, once to Teta, once to Bob and twice to Aunt Lorene. I have been very conscientous [sic] about writing because I know how you look forward to letters but I must say that I am a trifle discouraged.

You asked about Genevieve—I do not think that the big gun story is true because I have never heard of it and I am sure that if anything that exciting had happened we would know of it. She is still in Paris driving for the American Fund. Poor Kid—she was rather up against it because she had given her car and had also signed up as a Motor Driver so there was no way out for her. You see we had signed as motor mechanics so when they could not give us that sort of work to do we were free to leave. We could have stayed with them and driven in Paris as Genevieve is doing but if I wanted to do city driving I could do it in St. Paul.

If you could only see how cozy and comfortable we are in this little town you would not worry about us. Dode and I have a darling little room and Mugs has one in the house next door but we all eat here together. Our French maid is a jewel and I tell you that it is great to have a comfortable place and a good dinner waiting for us when we get home at night after working the way we do. We are only a block from the station and it takes us ten minutes by train to get to the first canteen [at Orry-la-Ville] or twenty to get to the second [at Survilliers]. The first is really the one we are stationed at but in rush times they send some of the workers to the second. I have been there for the past week, working from seven in the morning till six at night. It is some work I do tell you but we are delighted to be here and be able to do it. We served eight hundred meals this noon to say nothing of the millions of hard boiled eggs, sandwiches and cups of coffee sold on the side. The second canteen is the one that the soldiers pass thru on their way from the front to their homes when they start on their permission of leave and they are the happiest bunch that you have ever seen. They are cheerful at——when on their way back to the trenches, too, but it is a sort of brave cheerfulness that does not ring as true as the kind I have been seeing for the past week.

We all start to work together in the morning, buy the Paris Herald from the Frenchwoman who sells papers at the station, read the war news and the President's latest speech on the way down in the train, talk to any Americans that we chance to meet, arrive at the canteen, get into our aprons and veils and start on the day's work. The Poilus become more interesting every day.

I know that this is a bum letter but I am so tired that I can hardly see the keys so must close for tonight. I will not write long letters but I will try to write often. I noted what you said about coming home when my time was up but I do not think that there is much chance of that. Major Olds said just before we left Paris that he thought that it was up to the Americans in France to stay here and work like dogs until they did something before any of them started to think of going home. It really seems as tho it were up to them. However, we will wait and see how things turn out before we make any plans. Perhaps at the end of our three months here they will send us home as ones who have failed to make good. Over two hundred American women have had their passports recalled—you have to mind your Ps and Qs over here. Well, Love to all, write often and so will I.

Al.

8 July 1918
[Chantilly]

Dear Mama and all—

It is nine O'Clock, Dode is on night duty, so I am sitting up in our
little room all alone and am going to scratch you a line, by candle
light, before I turn to bed.

My job this week is that of Cashier. I go to work on the nine-thirty
train and return on the eight. Our biggest rush was at noon, today,
and after sitting in a hot little cashier's box and selling tickets to
seven-hundred and fifty men my head fairly swam with francs and
centimes.

Every time we see an American boy we speak to him and we have
met some very interesting ones since here. Miss Larabee knows an
aviateur, just happened to meet him on the train one day. Didn't
even know he was in France, who is attached to the famous French
escadrille of "Storks." He must be a promising flyer or they would
not put him in that escadrille as it is the most glorious air group in
France. The idolized Guynemer was a member of the "Storks" and
Fonck, the foremost French *Aviateur,* since Guynemer's death, now
leads the group.[72]

The American's name is [H.] Clay Ferguson, watch the papers and
you'll read of him unless he is killed before able to make a name for
himself. He is such a nice youngster and as I looked across the table
at him, he was here to dinner one night, I could not realize that he
had been across the lines that very morning and had battled with a
Hun plane. He drives a "Spad" machine, a fighting plane, and is in

---

72. Escadrille N3, also called the "Storks," was a well-known unit of
fighter pilots in the French military. Georges Guynemer and René Fonck
were ace pilots.

the most dangerous branch of the Avatier [*sic*].[73] I wish him luck!—
He knows his chances aren't worth much but he says that he is
going to fight like hell for as long as he lasts.

Well, no real news—I wrote to Nonie[74] the day before yesterday.
An American mail is about due so I'm expecting a letter.

Love to All,
Alice

~

13 July 1918
[Chantilly]

Dear Mama, Dad and All—

I have been too tired for the past four nights to even commence a
letter and I am so sleepy now that I can hardly see so this will [be] a
short one.

I had a slight abscess in my tooth, the other day, didn't ache at all
and it broke before I knew I had it but I thought I ought to see a
dentist, nevertheless, so went into Paris for the day. He said that
either a nerve had died or some food had slipt [*sic*] under the gum,
but, whatever the cause, all the trouble was over and I could let it go
for four or five months. On my return here, that night, I found three
welcome letters waiting for me, one from Mama, one from Jack and
one from Auntie Marie. Poor Jack!—All my sympathies are with

---

73. The SPAD was a French military biplane developed by the Société
Pour L'Aviation et ses Dérivés. It was flown by Guynemer, Fonck, and
American Eddie Rickenbacker.

74. Likely Alice's aunt Nora Mullery Lammers.

him but "It's the War."[75] Everyone suffers in war time, some thru actual pain, some thru bereavement and some thru disappointment. He is of the latter class and I don't know but what it is the hardest of all to stand up under. Oh well! It will all be over some day and then he'll be ahead of the game that he is in and all the rest will be behind.

Isn't it great that the Browns are returning with Auntie Marie? I do hope they'll enjoy the Houseboat. Does it leak this summer?— And Bob wants to go surveying—Good for him. Let him go when Lyman[76] learns—Too bad about the Cypress deal but tell Dad to remember that it's growing every day.[77] That's what he always used to say. When in Paris I left an order with Morgan-Harjes to send you a telegram on your birthday. I suppose you wondered about the queer wording of it but you see, you can't send a cable without your passport and, of course, I could not leave my military papers in Paris so I had to have them send it and sign it and say "Alice says, "Happy birthday,"—Hope you got it O.K.

---

75. The state department decreed that women volunteers could not have a father, son, husband, or brother in the armed services, though the opposite was not true. Alice, like many of her female friends, may have asked her brother Jack to defer enlisting until she had secured her own position. Through her letters, we learn that he was initially rejected by the draft board.

76. Alice's cousin, Lyman Brown, the son of Lorene Mullery and Robert Brown.

77. Likely the Burton-Schwartz agreement that Alice refers to in other letters.

THREE

Germany's Last Offensive

Throughout the spring, Ludendorff's strategy and success had not aligned. The Spring Offensive was intended to be a small diversion that would draw Allied troops away from the north, creating a weakened defense for a more effective assault toward the channel ports. To his surprise, his troops had made large and unexpected gains, creating a salient that threatened Paris, even as it was difficult to defend and supply. Ludendorff knew this bulge was a risk, yet he hoped one more diversion could draw his enemy's troops where he wanted them. In June, he began preparations for a final diversion. This battle of the Marne became a turning point in the war.[1]

~

16 July 1918
[Chantilly]

Dear Mama, Dad and all—

I started a letter to you three days ago and took it to the Canteen yesterday in hopes that I would have a minute to finish it but no such

---

1. Cruttwell, *History of the Great War*, 533–35.

luck. I left it there last night so I will write this now and send them along together.

We had a great time on your birthday, it is a great fete day in France and just like our Fourth of July. You remember, if you got the letter, that we invited the officers of the camp to dinner on the Fourth so they returned the courtesy and invited us to have dinner with them, at their mess, on the Fourteenth. We all went and had a gay time and when the dinner was all over we stood around the table and with raised glasses cried "Here's to Victory, Vive la France, Vive l'Amerique." Then we sang the national song of France and the Star Spangled Banner and I could hardly keep the tears from rolling down my face. On the way home we heard the distant booming of the cannons and the war seemed more hideous to me than it ever did before.[2] I told the French Lieutenant who sat next to me that it was your birthday so we had a little toast all to ourselves, wished you a long life and a merry one. Little did you know that a French officer was toasting you with real champagne somewhere in France, Hey?

We have been buying cigarettes from time to time, when we could get them, to take to the hospitals but they are so hard to get here that we wrote in to Major Olds and he had the Red Cross send us a crate of them to distribute as we saw fit. The crate was sent to France by the Tobacco Fund that is being raised in America thru the newspapers. I remember that the Pioneer Press was doing something about it just before I left home. It is a wonderful thing and the nicest of all about it is that the tobacco comes packed so attractively that it is like handing a sick soldier a Christmas Stocking. Each red, white

---

2. At midnight on July 14, Alice and her companions heard the sounds of the French cannons proactively bombing the German lines. The Allies were well aware that a new German offensive was to begin the next day, and indeed it did. The Second Battle of the Marne had commenced. Cruttwell, *History of the Great War*, 534.

and blue package contains two sacks of Bull Durham, one package of pipe tobacco and two packages of cigarettes. Inside of each box is a post card, stamped and addressed to the person who gave the money to the newspaper to add to the Fund. It is a wonderful idea and it would have done your heart good to see the cheer that went thru the wards when each man had a box on the bed beside him. It was not long before they had unpacked them to see what was at the bottom, just like kids, and before we had left most of them had written their thanks on the back of the postal cards and given them to us to mail. It was such a satisfaction to be able to give them enough to last awhile instead of walking from bed to bed and leaving only two or three cigarettes the way we have been doing. Lots of the boxes I handed out were from Minneapolis and one was from Duluth. When we finished at the tent hospital we went up to the Sister's and did the same thing for the wounded there. As we left we saw a one-armed man telling his comrade what to write on his card for him because he said that it had to go immediately to the kind American that it had come from. They needed some safety pins at the hospital so we went with them this morning and two of [the] men that we had been talking to the other day died last night. *"C'est la Guerre"* (It's the war, or that is what the war means).

I do not know when I am coming home but I have given up all idea of leaving here the first of September. I couldn't leave in the face of things. It would be like turning your back on suffering and running away. There is so much work to be done, they need American girls so badly and it is so terribly difficult to get them here. I hear that they are going to start a campaign in America for volunteer nurses, they need thousands of them and I guess there will be very few American girls crossing the pond towards New York this fall. America looks pretty good to me and I think I will fill the Harbour with tears of joy when I stand on the deck of the steamer that brings me in sight of the Statue of Liberty but I don't want to leave while I am needed here.

I did not receive the shoe strings that you write about but I can get them here when I need them.

The offensive is on again, started yesterday so we do not know much about it yet but we hear that it is not to the North of us as was expected but to the west.[3] I guess the Allies are ready for them but it will be a bad mess anyhow. The Hospitals will be crowded to the doors again and all France will suffer in sympathy for the wounded. I guess we will have one big battle after another until winter sets in and then—next spring—the Allies will march to Berlin.[4] We have not had many air raids lately and I don't know what it means unless what we hear is true and that is that the Allies have the mastery of the air. I hope that they can keep it and will bomb the devil out of the German towns and give them a dose of their own medicine.

We saw another bunch of prisoners yesterday and the most remarkable thing about them is that they smell to heaven. I think a German is some sort of human swine anyhow so perhaps they have a right to smell. A Poilu gave me a cane that he captured during an attack on the German trenches and, at present, it is my prize possesion [sic]. If I keep on adding to my collection I will have quite a bunch of souvenirs by the time I get to the U.S.A.

Well, must close now, the candle is flickering out and I am nodding with sleep. Mugs came into the room last night and saw me darning my socks by the feeble light and said that she realized, for

---

3. The German General Ludendorff intended the attack on the Marne to work as a diversion to draw Allied troops down from the north. Cruttwell, *History of the Great War*, 532.

4. At this point, no one predicted the war could possibly end in 1918. Optimists might hope that the Germans would retreat to the Hindenburg Line by winter, and the Allies were making plans for efforts the following spring. Cruttwell, *History of the Great War*, 547.

the first time, how far we were from home. You bet we're a long way off when I start darning.

Write soon, Love to you all,
Alice

~

[~19 July 1918]
[Chantilly]

Dear Mama and All—

Today was a big one for me because when I arrived at the Canteen I found six letters waiting for me. Two from Mama, one from Teta, one from Auntie Lorene, one from Max and one from Andrew Berkey. He had received my address from Minnie.[5] He has been promoted, is now a Lieutenant but in the South of France and crazy to get to the front. I would like to answer all your letters singly but I think the best plan is to write each letter to All. I would like to write Jack but hate to trust the Louisiana postmasters so send my letters to him when you have finished reading them.

The Browns and All of you must be spending your hot afternoons on the River Bank by this time. I sometimes wish that I had a cool bank to sit on as it has been as hot as Hades here for the past week. Our bathtub never works so the only kind of a bath we get is in a bowl of water. The St. Croix would feel good to me right this minute. We are having a few dull days at the Canteen because all the Soldiers are kept at their posts while the Big Battle is on. The Germans pushed for Paris for the fifth time but were "foiled again."

---

5. Likely Minnie Comstock.

We just heard of the Splendid French and American attacks on Soissons and are unspeakably happy over it.[6] All the Hospitals are packed to the doors again. We heard last night that three American boys were wounded and at a French Hospital in our town so we are going over to cheer them up a bit. It is pretty hard on them to be down and out and not able to talk the language. We also hear that an American Field Hospital is to settle near us so we will have to do what we can for the boys that come there. Everyone is crazy about the way the "Yanks" are fighting and they say that the Germans are scared to death when they know that they are in the trenches opposite them. A French officer told us that he had seen men of all the Allied Nations fighting but he had never seen any men fight the way the Americans do. They are simply crazy mad at the Germans and when they start nothing can hold them back. I suppose we will see lots of German prisoners in the next few days and we are all looking forward to it with great *glee*. We gloat over every one we see.

I have told you, but perhaps you did not receive the letter, that Genievive [*sic*] Washburn is still in Paris with the A.F.F.W.—She came over as a driver so of course is doing what she expected to do. I saw her the day I went into Paris. She is hale and hearty, her car has not yet arrived but she is driving one of the French cars. She is going to stay with them for six months and then is going to look for something more interesting. Perhaps she will go to Italy as her brother is in Rome with the American Red Cross.

Max wrote that he called and found you all at home and that Dad was still saying that I had no business in France. I wish he could see me for about twelve hours out of the twenty-four and he might change his mind.

---

6. On July 18, the Allies struck a counteroffensive on the western front of the German's salient between Soissons and Château-Thierry. Johnson, *1918: The Unexpected Victory*, 81.

Ruth[7] wrote to Dode that she was coming over in the Fall and we are all jubilant over that. I am glad that you are getting my letters and it is nice when you mention a certain thing I wrote about because then I know what letter you have received. You mentioned my Hospital Experience so I know that you received the letters I wrote just before leaving Paris.

(time to go home now—I will finish this tomorrow)

(Next Day)

Our days are so full that it is hard to tell just what to write about. Last night, when we got home, we found word waiting for us that the wounded were pouring into the four Hospitals of the town and to come over and lend a hand. We went over and took with us fruit, cigarettes and Eggs. They were the men that had made the wonderful attack to the North of us, in fact the Battle is still going on, and the men are pouring in like a stream. We have decided to double up for a few days—half of us work at the Canteen and half at the Hospitals, taking turns. It will be hard work for awhile but everyone feels that you can't work hard enough these days. Especially after seeing and talking to the boys from the trenches and knowing how they suffer. No matter how we work, our lot is an easy one compared to theirs. The boys are so unselfish that it is sweet to see them. One nice young kid from Indiana said that he was not badly wounded so to take some of the other fellows first and when they took the bandage off of his eye, instead of finding the flesh wound they expected they found his left eye shot away. He said that he was lucky not to have lost more than that.—They put up a wonderful fight and all France is feeling gay over their success. One American looked and talked so much like Uncle John[8] that I thought I was in Duluth. It is

---

7. Ruth Kellogg, Doris Kellogg's sister.

8. Alice's uncle John C. Mullery lived and worked in Duluth in the family lumber business.

awful to see them stretched out in rows on the ground, outside the Field Hospital, waiting for attention. It seems funny to me that there are not more Doctors than there are.

Well, will close now. It is as hot as the very D- here today, terribly windy and the air foggy with dust, there is so much traffic on the roads.

Love to All,
Alice
P. S. This is the kind of paper we give to the Soldiers at the Canteen. Beautiful, isn't it?

~

[~20 July 1918]
[Canteen, Orry-la-Ville]

Dear Mama, Dad, The Browns, and All the rest—

I am insulted because ever since we have had the Houseboat I have wanted the Browns to visit us but they waited till I got to France to go. Can it be that the possibility of Air Raids in New York made Minnesota look more than ordinarily good to them?

I am writing on the kind of paper that we give to the Poilus as I am at the Canteen and there is nothing else about to scribble on. We have been rushed to death for the past week, working a good, stiff, twelve hours a day. Yesterday noon we gave regular full sized meals to eight hundred and fifty men. It took us three and one half hours to serve them. They come up for their trays a la Cafeteria and by the time eight hundred of them pass by you feel that you are feeding the entire Army. There were six thousand men in Camp yesterday and it was a wonderful sight to see them.

I had such a nice letter from Nonie yesterday. It was written on the eleventh of June but she did not say whether or not the long spell was broken and that you had heard from me. I do hope so. It is so discouraging to write when you feel your letters never get thru. Ed wrote that he had written before but I never received the letter or letters so I know some of my mail is going astray but the more you write the more I'll get so keep at it. Send me some pictures of you all on board the "Ripple."

The train we expect is almost due—

The train came and with it about two thousand men. Things were very busy for about five hours but we are all through now and are about ready to take the train home. We work like nailers[9] but I can't tell you how happy it makes you feel to crawl into bed at night, tired as possible, but knowing that you have really done something worth while. There is a lot more to do before the war will be over but each day brings us just that much nearer to the goal. We Americans are lucky when you think that the French and English have been "Carrying On" for four years and are going to stick to see the finish. Every hale and hearty man in France is wearing the Colors and most of the poor souls have left large families behind when they left home for the trenches.

We saw seven hundred German Prisoners the other afternoon— the mud of the trenches still clinging to their clothes. Most of them were surprisingly young or old. I guess their first Army is about done for.[10] They were badly dressed, no wool in their uniforms, and their feet were poorly shod. They can't look too badly to suit me. I would like to see them in rags & tags and starving to

---

9. To "work like nailers" meant to work extremely hard.

10. Alice's observation and her surmising were remarkably accurate. Germany had essentially run out of conscripts. Cruttwell, *History of the Great War,* 522.

The crowds of soldiers at the camp were large. This photo shows a group of over fifty men outside a canteen, likely Canteen #2, located at Survilliers.

death.[11] The things I have heard about them, from people who *know*, are enough to make your hair curl. Everyone is waiting for the next offensive but the armies of the Allies are laying for them and their progress will be slight, I'm sure. They are buying real estate at a terrific price and, when they get played out, Foch will turn on them and give them Hell.

I was very disappointed to hear that the Cypress deal did not go thru but the war will be over some day and then "Watch us grow."[12] It will be a big day when "Johny [*sic*] comes Marching Home" but

---

11. Alice's unpleasant desires were pretty much coming true. By the summer of 1918, the Royal Navy's blockade of German ports had struck a serious blow to the nation's food supply. Civilians were near starvation, and both civilian and military support for the war was waning. Johnson, *1918: The Unexpected Victory*, 123.

12. Likely the Burton-Schwartz agreement that Alice refers to in other letters.

Camp life outside the canteen, likely at Survilliers.

until then, I guess, we'll all have to buckle down and face things. America hasn't been touched yet and she will never suffer the way France has, her men and women killed, country devastated, children mutilated, Towns and Cathedrals ruined, beautiful forests razed to the ground, and all for the sake of German ambitions. However, the future of Germany looks as bad as their famous cheese smells and they have themselves to thank for it.

Well—will stop now—write soon—Love to you all. Poor Bob, he'll have to slave all alone over the engine on the Houseboat this summer. Maybe you can train Lyman in as an Assistant Engineer Bob! Hope Florence[13] will run the Electric. Her motoring carreer [*sic*] should be started immediately. If you could see the quantities of fresh eggs we handle (Mama and Auntie Marie referred to) your

---

13. Alice's cousin Florence Brown would have been turning sixteen this month. Electric cars were considered more suitable for women, as they were cleaner and slower and could not go as far as gasoline-engine cars.

heads would swim. When I think of you scouring the countryside for a case of eggs I look at our two thousand or so and *smile*.

Love to all,
Alice

~

25 July 1918
[Chantilly]

Dear Mama, Dad and all—

This is just a short note because I have no time for a real letter.

Enclosed is a snap shot taken of Mugs, Dode and myself talking to a bunch of typical Poilus and giving them coffee out of one of the windows of the canteen. If we could send you a picture with five thousand of them around the canteen, the scene would be more realistic. A woman came out from Paris and took some photographs for the R.C. yesterday and I will send you a set if I can get a hold of them.

We have been very busy with the wounded lately. Poor boys they need all the attention they can get. A nice boy, one whom we are all interested in, died and his funeral was one of the saddest things I have ever attended. He was buried with full military honors but the army is too busy with the *Grand Attaque* to do much else so the Military Honors consisted of a handful of French Guards, a French and American flag and a procession made up of two nurses, four of us, some French and a couple of Doctors. He was buried with six others and I couldn't help thinking how six American families longed to be in France that day.

Love to you all—write often
Alice
We all are well—

~

28 July 1918
[Chantilly]

Dear Mama, Dad and All—

Life goes on about the same. We are very busy at the Canteen, big crowds, and put in all our extra time at the Hospitals. The fly season is here and, I regret to say, the French fly is even more persistent than his American brother. It's all we can do to keep them out of the food—they are simply disgusting—and it is pathetic to see the poor wounded in the hospitals, simply covered with them. Of course, it is impossible to keep them out of the tent hospitals and the poor boys soon get exhausted trying to drive them off so they patiently suffer them to crawl all over their faces.

The young American that I wrote about before [H. Clay Ferguson], the Aviator, was here again yesterday with thrilling tales to tell. He is such a nice boy, we are all interested in him, and hate to think that it is too much to hope that he will survive the war. He is in the most dangerous branch of the Aviation and it will be a marvel if he skins thru. He said that he was going to bring Fonck, the famous French "Ace" to dinner some night so that will be interesting.[14] Bobbett was here for a day, on an inspection trip, and said that it was the best day he spent in France. He has been bottled up in Paris so found things here most interesting.

We have had a lot of cloudy weather lately, no air raids, lots of sleep and are in the pink of condition. We love the rain as it lays the dust which is almost unbearable in dry weather. The traffic is so heavy that the air gets cloudy with it, it's like working in a flour mill some days.

---

14. Colonel René Fonck (1894–1953) was the top air fighter not just for France but for all the Allied powers. He was rather busy this July, shooting down seven enemy planes.

They (the Red Cross) need Americans so badly that there is some talk of recalling all the girls that are in French Canteens and sending them to American Posts. It really seems the right thing to do but we would all hate to leave here as we have become so interested in the things surrounding us. Alice Lee Herrick, the girl that was engaged to Dick Myers,[15] arrived in France and Mugs saw her the day she was in Paris. She is going to work in one of the R.C. recreation huts at an American Base Hospital. Major Olds says that the R.C. wants to cable for a lot of the right sort of girls and wants us to suggest some names of girls in St. Paul. We will try to get Mary Morrissey[16] over but, as her brother is in the army, it is rather doubtful. We shall also try for Agnes Morrison,[17] A. Warren[18] is too young, and I shall speak of the two Kavanaugh girls.[19] They would have their expenses paid so if they get a cable tell them to come along. It's great over here. Ruth Kellogg is coming over early in the fall and Dode has written her asking her to bring the things to me that you send to her—805 Delaware Ave. Please send the following, and only the following, as her baggage will be restricted.

12 pairs of silk stockings—size 10

3 pairs of heavy, one button gloves—size 7

---

15. Alice Lee Herrick (1891–) and Richard Meyers (1889–) were from Chicago. After the war they did marry, and were living in Paris in 1923 when their son was born.

16. Mary R. Morrissey (1893–) served in France with the Red Cross from November 1918 to June 1919.

17. Agnes Morrison (1893–) first traveled to France in November 1916 to work for the American Committee of Fatherless Children in France. She stayed there until November 1917. She returned again in December 1918 to work as a "Confidential stenographer" to the military attaché in Brussels, and returned to St. Paul in September 1919.

18. Likely Alice Warren (1895–1982), sister of Alvah H. Warren Jr.

19. Possibly Mary G. Kavanaugh and her family in St. Paul.

1 pair of black, low heeled Oxford—size 6-B—and my black fur coat. I'll probably never wear the latter but I am afraid to lose the good chance of getting it here.

I could, if necessary, get all the above here but they cost like the devil and wear out in a flash. Especially shoes.

Budge has been kind enough to send us the Literary Digest so don't mind sending that but ship along the New Republic now and then.

In buying the shoes please try to get the long vamp flat-heeled kind that I have been wearing lately. Mrs. Bend will know if you don't remember.

Well—must go to dinner now—I could eat the table cloth. We have all we want to eat, meat, butter, sugar, etc.—don't need a thing.

Love to All,
"Al"

⁓

31 July 1918
[Chantilly]

Dear Jack—

I have been meaning to write for some time but whenever we take the time to write a letter it's like stealing it. We are either neglecting work or rest and it's between the devil and the deep sea to choose between the two evils as both have a strong appeal these days.

Mama wrote that you were thinking of coming over with the Red Cross so I thought I'd write you and say how I think things stand over here. All the soldiers seem to have a great respect for the Red Cross but seem to resent seeing so many young men among the personel [*sic*]. I think, myself, that a good bunch of them are slackers but also know that a lot of them, like yourself, can show their draft board refusals but they are not always given the benefit of the doubt which is not at all fair but "*C'est la Guerre.*" I have talked to many wounded soldiers in the Hospitals and around about and they speak of the Red Cross men (the healthy ones) as "Bummies." If you could come over and be sure of getting a real job in a front line Canteen or driving a R.C. Ambulance it would be worth the racket but otherwise I would rather you stay in the U.S. and fill a man's sized job as you are doing. The Red Cross has plenty of Bank presidents in France and a lot of them have been here for a long time so have first shot at the interesting jobs. The chances are that if you came over you would be kept either in Paris, attached to an American Base Hospital in Southern France or drive a truck for a Canteen. We have two cars here, one attached to each Canteen, but I can not imagine you satisfied with a job such as our chauffeurs have. Our Chauffer [*sic*] is good because, at present, I am one of them. The driver of the Ford at Canteen #2 went on a spree and was peremptorily dismissed so I am filling his shoes.

Do not know yet whether they are going to send us another man or send me a license and don't much care which they do. It has been interesting for me, have had the opportunity of seeing a lot of the Country, but driving a grocery wagon over dusty hot roads does get tiresome. You fall in line behind a convoy and swallow dust for an hour.

The chauffeur at No. 1 is a nice boy named Potter. Went to St. Pauls & knows nice people—has eye trouble so is in the R.C. He is not a very adventerous [*sic*] soul and has a girl in the vicinity so seems quite satisfied with life. I don't want to be discouraging but at the same time want you to be wise and not be disappointed later. Above all else don't come with the Y.M.C.A.—I understand that they offer alluring prospects in the States but they don't look good to me.

Had a letter from Andrew and he is in Bordeaux, way down South, and has been there ever since landing in France. They are constructing docks down there. He is wild with impatience and is trying to get transferred into the tank Service but not much chance. Al Warren has been at the front but was at an Artillary [*sic*] school the last I heard. Did you ever know Bob Browning[20] of Minneapolis? We had luncheon with him when we were in Paris and heard just the other day that he was a prisoner in Germany. They say that he ran out of gas while flying over enemy lines. Sounds like him.

Well—must close—They are calling to go home so I'll go out and start the little truck. There's not a tight nut on it and when we rattle over the rough roads I have to keep my teeth clamped or I would lose my expensive gold inlays.

Love to all and lots to yourself. I know that it's terribly hard to be in your position—much harder than going to the trenches I think— But everyone understands and, at least, you're doing your bit for American Industry and that is what is going to win the war. Everyone is a soldier these days but I bet a hat Mama isn't keeping meatless, wheatless days.

Love again,
"Al"

~

4 August 1918
[Chantilly]

Dear Mama, Dad, and All—

I couldn't possibly tell you how happy I am this morning. Isn't the War news wonderful! Soissons captured, the Huns driven back

---

20. Robert George Browning (1892–) was captured in Cochem, Germany, on July 10, 1918.

across the Vesle and their whole offensive and their ridiculous hopes dashed to the ground.[21] France is wild with joy today. All the farm people have smiles on their faces and the poor patient French Soldier sees, for the first time, Victory and Piece [*sic*] in view. All the girls are clapping each other on the back this morning and moving about their work with smiles on their faces that won't come off.

The American boys are truly marvelous fighters, the truth of it is borne in on us every day, and they are the admiration of the Allied world. Their spirit is unmatchable and they go "over the top and at them" Just as tho they were in a football game.

I have a new job—chauffeur at Canteen No. #2. The last chauffeur went on a bat and was fired and as they are very scarce in France the R.C. sent word that it would be some time before they could replace him. In the meantime I was to run the car. Mrs. Church said that everything was so satisfactory that she was going to ask Major Osborn for a permit for me to continue as chauffeur. I was quite willing so everything has been arranged. When we were in Paris with the A.F.F.W. we set up in a Ford Chassis for the same Major Osborn[22] so when Mrs. Church asked for my permit he consented

---

21. Since the Allied counterattack began July 18, the German salient was weakening significantly. After the Allied capture of Château-Thierry on July 21, the Germans began to consider a strategic retreat in order to straighten out and strengthen their line. This retreat was to begin on the night of August 1, but the plans were foiled by an Allied attack that began that morning. By evening the French cavalry had reached the outskirts of Soissons. On August 2, the Germans withdrew from Soissons, and by the next day they had retreated across the Vesle River. The German losses from these battles, collectively known as the Marne, were 100,000, including 35,000 prisoners, and 650 guns. Johnson, *1918: The Unexpected Victory*, 82–83; Cruttwell, *History of the Great War*, 543.

22. C. G. Osborn of Chicago was director of transportation for the Red Cross in France.

In August 1918, Alice began to shift from canteen work to driving a supply truck for the camps. "I have been thankful, many times for the rain coat you pressed me to buy at Abercrombie's. It is useful for rain & dust as well and oh! The dust!!"

COURTESY OF ROBIN BROOKSBANK

without a moment's hesitation as he remembered my name. He has always been prejudiced against women drivers and everyone said that he would never have them in his department but evidently he has changed his mind. Perhaps has been forced into doing it. However, I am a Chauffeur—have been for the past two weeks and it is very interesting as I see so much of the surrounding country. My car is a Ford truck, carries a ton, and as I go along the roads with carrots, turnips, raw meat, sacks of coffee, etc., sticking out behind, I feel exactly like an Army supply wagon driver which, of course, indirectly, I am. All the Soldiers on the road salute me and my hand is in the air, waving back a greeting, almost as often as when I drive out Summit Avenue in the old gray Packard.

Mrs. Church and I drive to a little town nearby to market, about twice a week, and it is an interesting sight. The square in the old town is packed with people walking from booth to booth and the air is shrill with the cries of the market women advertising their wares. All the Military Cars in the district go there for rations and it is like a huge Quartermaster's department. Then we go to the French Army abbatoir [sic] and after about half an hour's red tape regarding permits, IOUs, military privileges, etc., we get our load of meat, usually five hundred pounds of beef or mutton, and then we come rattling home past Aviation Fields, barb wire entanglements, searchlight divisions, army railroads, temporary telegraph communications, anti-aircraft guns, listening posts, camauflaged [sic] barracks and all sorts of interesting things with always a couple of hospitals thrown in and the road crowded with ambulances and all sorts of military traffic, sometime full regiments of marching men. As we go past they often cry "Les Americanes" [sic] and give us a cheer. It's wonderful and I wouldn't miss it for anything in the world.

So glad you received my Cable, and on time too,—One of the letters you didn't get must have been the one with a map of the Canteen drawn on the back. The censors hate maps of any sort. Well—love to All—had three letters from you (Mama) yesterday and they made me feel awfully happy. Don't worry about my health. On my word of honor I am *perfectly* well, eat lots and am not thin. Work agrees with me.

Love again,
Alice

~

[~6 August 1918]
[Chantilly]

Dear Mama, Dad and All—

Nothing particular to write about but think I will send this off just so that you will get a letter.

I am chauffeur now and busy every day getting my load at the markets and getting it to the canteen in time to feed the Poilus. Just to give you an idea of the quantities we deal in—the following is an ordinary day's purchases—one thousand eggs, five hundred pounds of meat, five hundred heads of lettuce, fifty heads of cabbage, four hundred peaches, two hundred of loaves of bread and all the other stuff that we receive from the Red Cross warehouses in Paris and that they ship us by railroad. It is a big job to get all the food that we need to feed as many men as we do and when I get home I think that I will be able to market for the crowds on the houseboat without turning a hair.

Lucile[23] is at her job and her unit is in southern France and she says that things are very quiet down there. Alice Lee Herrick was detailed to open a recreation hut at a base hospital and imagine her joy when she got to her post to find that Lucile was there. Wasn't that a piece of luck. Mugs received a letter from Wallace[24] who is with an amunition [sic] train and in the south for the time being but soon expects to get to the trenches. Of course, we have not seen Lucile and don't know when we will. Mugs may be able to meet her in Paris for a day two weeks from now but she will not be able to get out here and see us at work. It is a rare thing to have callers in the war zone.

---

23. Marguerite Davis's sister Lucile Davis (1884–) served with the US Medical Corps and Red Cross in France.

24. Marguerite Davis's brother Wallace Davis served with the army from August 1918 to July 1919.

Alice in a quiet moment, resting on the running board of her Ford truck.

The country around here is simply beautiful, lovely parks, two wonderful forests, several chateaus, and the cunningest little villages you can imagine. Every town has its quaint old church and market place, you must come over and see France when the war is over. For the past few days we have seen refugees passing thru on their way up to the country which has recently been liberated.[25] It is such a happy sight to see them returning to their homes and such a sad sight to see them being driven out. I tell you things are very different since the last Allied victory and a happy end is looming in sight for all. The country people around here were all ready to leave at a moment's notice a few weeks ago but now they are happy again and have settled down to their usual existence.

We visit the hospitals regularly and do what we can for the boys. One of them died last night and we are all so sad over it. I wish I had

---

25. The Marne pocket which had been liberated was between Soissons and Rheims.

known that young Hines was sick over here and where he was and I might have been able to see him. The Red Cross is very considerate about that sort of thing. If you know of any one, any time, that you want me to look up cable me and I will do what I can.

Well, must close now—I hear that we can have things sent to us if we have our demands checked by a bureau over here so if I need things I will send you a letter which will advise the post office to accept them for shipment. Did you send the things I asked you to [give] to Ruth Kellogg to bring over. In case you did not receive the letter I will ask over again—twelve pairs of black silk stockings size ten—my black fur coat—black oxfords—and I think that's all.

Love again
Alice

FOUR

The Beginning of the End

At the start of August, the Allied forces were celebrating their recent successes in the Marne pocket between Soissons and Château-Thierry, but victory was still not assured. Like other volunteers and soldiers near the front, Alice and her fellow canteen workers tried to gauge the status of the war through reading papers, sharing conversations, and observing the evidence of war: wounded soldiers returning from the front, planes buzzing above or shot down, prisoners of war, and airfields and hospitals sprouting up.

Lundendorff's confidence in his army remained high. Suspecting that the Allies might attack again, on August 4 he issued an order of the day that "we should wish for nothing better than to see the enemy launch an offensive, which we can but hasten the disintegration of his forces."[1] Two days later, on August 6, the Germans attacked south of Morlancourt and briefly reclaimed territory that had been lost on July 29. A day later, the Allies seized it again. It appeared that the balance of power might seesaw between the two sides.

But just one day later, on August 8, the Allies struck a critical blow to the Germans at Amiens, creating what Lundendorff called "the black day of the German army." Though the German casualties of

---

1. Johnson, *1918: The Unexpected Victory*, 92.

the battle were modest by World War I standards (28,000), and the number of German prisoners taken similarly modest (15,000), too, the morale of the Germany army was crumbling. Large groups of German soldiers had surrendered to single troops or isolated squadrons. Replacement troops were heckled by retiring troops and jeered for prolonging the fight. Soldiers ignored their officers' orders.[2] Over the next few days, the Allies continued beating back the Germans.

By August 13, Lundendorff had concluded that it was no longer possible for the Germans to win the war. His forces were too weak and demoralized, and the numbers of Americans too great. The German lines were awkwardly drawn and poorly fortified.[3] At a conference in Spa, he, the Chancellor Georg von Hertling, Field Marshal Paul von Hindenburg, and the secretary of state agreed it was time to negotiate for peace. The following day, Kaiser Wilhelm agreed.[4] For now, the Germans would try to straighten their lines and prevent further significant retreat, hoping to present a powerful enough threat to negotiate a fair peace.[5]

The Germans now knew they couldn't win, but they didn't yet know they might lose. The Allies, meanwhile, were prepared to fight to the end.

~

15 August 1918
[Chantilly]

Dear Mama, & Dad & All—

At the Canteen, sitting on a high stoop near the counter and looking out over our *refectorie* where a scattering of Poilus are eating their

---

2. Johnson, *1918: The Unexpected Victory*, 102.
3. Cruttwell, *History of the Great War*, 551.
4. Johnson, *1918: The Unexpected Victory*, 112.
5. Cruttwell, *History of the Great War*, 551.

evening meal. The train schedule has been recently changed so we have only a few men for supper but we still continue to hold our own for the rest of the day. We went "over the top" and broke our record the other day when we served nine-hundred and thirty meals in three hours.

You perhaps have read of the wonderful work the Scottish women have done in connection with the British Army and of their Hospital. We drove over to see it the other day and, all in all, it is quite the most interesting of all the Hospitals I have seen. There is not a man employed on the place, girl ambulance drivers, nurses, orderlies, cooks, and surgeons. One of the Surgeons is quite a genius and is considered one of the finest operators in France, barring none. The men are wonderfully cared for and are just as happy and contented as they can be, or as their wounds will permit. Each bed has a cheerful bright red coverlet over it and all the Pajama & Bathrobes that the men wear are made alike and with a little piping of red. You can't imagine how little details like that cheer up a Hospital. I said that there was not a man on the place but I forgot the Chef.—he is the one and only but he is well worth making an exception for. All dressed in white, five minutes before the nurses distribute the dinners, he marches out into a great court in the center of the building, and pipes a gay, shrill little tune on his fife and you should hear the roar of voices and the clapping of hands that answers to his call. The Hospital is in the old abbey of Royamont [*sic*], part of which was destroyed in the Revolution and the ruined walls still stand as a reminder of the other times and other wars.[6] I wonder if the world will ever get along without fighting.

Quite in contrast was another Hospital in a town near here. It is run by the order of St. Vincent, very clean and all that, but it is in

6. A Scottish Women's Hospital was located at the Royaumont Abbey from January 1915 to March 1919. The hospital was established by Elsie Maud Inglis, a pioneer surgeon and woman's rights advocate.

an old battered building that was an old man's home before the war and it has a blue, lonesome air about it that won't wash out. It is run entirely for & by the French and the poor Gov't. has so many of them all over the Country that some are bound to be neglected. This outfit is so poor that they seem to be scraping along and no more and the men were as happy as Children with the good things we brought them. Some of the old men are still hanging around and they lapped up the Hot Chocolate like—well—I hate to say dogs but that was the only thing that one poor old soul reminded me of.—We are going again *soon*.

We have had several *Boche* planes over us lately and in broad daylight. They are trying to sneak back over the lines and find out where Foch has his reserves massed. It is very exciting to see one in the air and the Anti-aircraft shells popping all around him. They look like pieces of white pop corn against the blue sky. All during the last two wonderful attacks and victories of the Allies we have heard the roar of the guns day and night, more insistant [*sic*] and oftener than usual. It is an ominous sound to go to sleep to but you get just as used to it as to everything else in life. Now that the Allies have pushed the line back we do not hear the cannon as loudly as we used to. Soon we will feel out of things entirely but they can't go far enough ahead to suit us. We eat, sleep, dream and eat war and we're as happy as anyone on earth over the last offensive—no flies on *Foch*—he is the idol of France now.

Well—must close—no more writing paper around. Received a letter from Bob & one from Mama today—delighted—but you spoke of writing three the preceeding [*sic*] week so I suppose I'll get these tomorrow. Love to all—you must be enjoying the St. Croix.

Love,
"Al"

18 August 1918
[Chantilly]

Dear Mama, Dad & All—

I have been so busy that I have not had time to write for five or six days. The last letter I wrote was after visiting the Scottish Hospital so hope you received it. Received a letter from Bob the other day. It was very nice to hear from him. Where is my old car? Is anyone using it this summer or is it sold or what? Maybe it would be wise to let Joy have it and I will get something new on my return.[7] He ought to give us about fourteen or fifteen hundred for it on a trade. Did the Joys ever get the letter I wrote to them? Did Louise F.? Did Dad get the one I sent to Jacksonville?

Aren't things going wonderfully over here. It must of been thrilling the day all the whistles & bells in America blew and rang over the capture of Soissons. How like America—It wasn't celebrated here at all—only with smiles and happy feelings. We are awfully busy these days. The Allied Armies are full of activity and I guess *Foch* is making his mark on the Germans. We have many many men in camp each day and, since the recent success, they go to the front with new hope in their hearts. What Bob wrote in his letter was right, "It is a great thing to be an American in France today." I had to go to a town, not far from here, the other day to buy two thousand eggs, (only a few hey?) and took Dode and a girl named Mitchell[8] with me. While there we went up to see the wonderful old Cathedral, one of the oldest in France, and as there were some things we wanted to know about the old glass windows, we went up to a nun, who was

7. Likely Joy Brothers Motor Car Company, owned by brothers Charles P. and Samuel J. Joy. The 1917 Polk City Directory shows they had an office and salesroom at Pleasant Avenue and Fourth and a garage on North Fourth, St. Paul.

8. Marguerite Mitchell (1882–1970) was from Brooklyn, New York.

Alice's food ration card classified her as a "T," war worker, giving her access to greater rations of bread, meat, and wine. Her occupation is listed as "chauffeur automobile."

working near the Altar, and asked her to tell us. She was very cool at first, thought we were English, but when she saw the U.S. on our shoulders she couldn't be nice enough. She broke into English and told us all about herself—She is *Irish,* born in Country [*sic*] Clare, and when she found out that my name was O'Brien and that I was from American-Irish, the Cathedral and all in it was ours for the asking. We had such a nice talk with her, she was full of fun, a regular rebel like Sister Clementine, and it's so nice to meet a stranger who talks English. You are drawn to them immediately.

They sent us an Ice Cream freezer from Paris so, the other day, three of us shared for two hours making chocolate Ice Cream with

Condensed Milk, Cocoa and a small amount of Sugar but my! it did taste good. When I get back to America I think I'll faint with joy at the sight of a chocolate Soda. Tell Bob to toss off a few and think of me.

We get all the food we want because we can pay for it but I do feel sorry for the Poor people who are living on next to nothing. Eggs cost one dollar a dozen, Butter is the same price per pound, jam costs ninety cents a pound—chicken is entirely out of the question—fruit is terribly expensive and of course flour and sugar are rationed so everyone has the same amount. Not all the money in the world would buy an extra pound. Of course, we get sugar from the Canteen and also grease, for cooking, so do not have to worry but I tell you, it is pretty hard on some people.

I shall have myself and my truck snapped some day and send it to you. I have been thankful, many times for the rain coat you pressed me to buy at Abercrombie's. It is useful for rain & dust as well and oh! The dust!! It's a regular nightmare but I don't give a damn or neither does anyone else because we're going to win the war—*surely*.

They're going to beat the hell out of the Germans some time soon! Nothing but profanity expresses jubilation.

Love to all
Al

~

28 August 1918
[Chantilly]

Dear Mama, Dad and All—

I am so happy because my mail has been arriving regularly. In the past ten days I have had four letters from home, one from Bob, one from Lyman, one from Auntie Marie and one from Lorene. Mrs. Bend has been a peach about writing us newsy letters. Every mail boat carries one addressed to Mugs and myself. It is so nice of her. I wish I could write to many people more often than I do but we are so busy that I simply haven't got the time. I am kept on the jump every minute, in my little Ford truck, buying vegetables, eggs, meat and food of all sorts and in odd minutes, taking things to the Hospitals in the vicinity. The American wounded always greet us with a cheer when we arrive. Poor Fellows!—If we could only do more for them. It is so hard to talk to the ones fatally wounded. You know that there is no hope for them but you have to lie cheerily and cheer them up if you can. I have seen many Minnesota boys in the Hospitals but have not run across any that I know. We visit the Scottish Woman's Hospital frequently and I can not say what wonderful work they do. The men that fall into their hands are lucky. The other day we visited their Chapel (you know the Hospital is in an old Abbey) and before the little Altar, rested three pine board Coffins covered with Flags, a French one on each side and an American in the center. His name was Petersen,[9] from North Dakota, and I had talked to him many times while he was lying in bed, looking out over the Court and longing for America. He died from abdominal wounds, a piece of shrapnel ploughed thru his side. I am glad that I am young and full of hope for the future or the present would be too much for me.

I am about to celebrate my twenty-seventh birthday—Think of it—I'll soon be too old for Military Service—Dode is giving a dinner and inviting all the workers (about twenty of us) and I am going to have a cake with Candles and *real* Ice Cream. Champagne too, no doubt, and we will drink to the health of all at home.

All your letters carry messages of Sympathy such as—I must be working so hard—not enough food—not enough sleep—feet must be sore, etc, etc. I am sorry if my letters have given you that impression because it is not a true one. Of course we do work hard but we

---

9. Likely Charlie Petersen (1894–1918).

love it and nothing is as healthy as hard work. We have fine beds and, I assure you, we use them a lot. I have never been better in my life—*never*—and I have everything I need. What do you know about Ruth Kellogg. She wrote us that she was coming over and the next thing we knew Dode received a Cable saying that she was engaged to a Captain Terry.[10] He is an Englishman, worse luck, and Dode hardly knows him. She is wild to be in America for the wedding but, of course, that cannot be. C'est la Guerre! So don't send the things to her to bring over as I don't think she will come. The orders about packages to the A.E.F. have been changed so whenever we need anything we can write an *approved* letter and that will be sufficient for the Postal Authorities to accept the package for shipment.

I received a very nice letter from Mrs. Donnelly—tell her that I shall answer it soon.

The Red Cross is about to start a Woman's Motor Service which makes it just that much harder to choose what to do next. There are so many jobs over here that I would like to tackle and the head of every department begs you to work for her or him so I guess I will close my eyes and jump. Dode and I are going to Paris tomorrow— just for the day—as we have some things to attend to. I shall see Major Olds about Jack.—Love to you all—

I haven't used the typewriter much lately because I write whenever I get a chance—I am at Canteen #2 now and just about to return to No. 1 with a load of supplies.[11] Had a successful morning as I managed to buy five hundred heads of lettuce and 2 thousand eggs.

Love
Alice

~

---

10. George S. Terry (1889–).

11. Canteen No. 1 was in Orry-la-Ville, and Canteen No. 2 was in Survilliers.

30 August 1918
[Chantilly]

Dear Mama, Dad & All—

I only wrote you the day before yesterday but I have so much news that I must write again. To begin with—we thought we were settled here for at least another two months but received a letter from Mrs. Vanderbilt yesterday, ordering us to Toul. It is an American Canteen, right in the heart of the American activities, and a privilege to be there as it is one of the most interesting of all the Canteens and, I am told, the town is fascinating. You see, they want all the younger American Girls with the Am. Troops, on account of the nutty age limit of the passport regulations, they have a lot of old Hens over here who should be home taking in Sewing.—Really it's disgusting. Of course, we leave here with great regret—we like all the girls and Mrs. Church so much—and we have had a wonderful summer. I would not have missed it for anything in the world but, at the same time, we are not loathe to take a whack at Toul.

Mugs, Dode and I are to go and perhaps a Miss Larrabee, from Amsterdam, New York, who we like very much.

1 Sept 1918

I started this letter two days ago but had to drop it so will finish it now.—As I said, we are going to Toul—expect to leave here in about two weeks, will be in Paris for about two days and are then going to take our vacation of a week in some quiet restful spot in the Country. Mrs. Vanderbilt makes all her girls take a permission every three months so they haven't a chance to get tired out. We think we will go to Brittany—Dode, Mugs, Pete Tenney, Lois Brundred, and myself. It is one of the most beautiful and quaintest spots in France and I think we would enjoy it immensely.—I can not believe that we have been here for almost three months and away from America for over five—Time flies!!—And over here things are so gripping that weeks pass by like half-hours at home.

We (Dode and I) were in Paris yesterday, signing our new papers, etc., and we had dinner with Mr. & Mrs. Olds. I talked to him about Jack but he was not very encouraging. He says that the Red Cross has passed a rule that they will not use any men of draft age—no matter whether or not they are refused by draft board. He said that they had to do it because the French did not understand having young men over here who were not with the Army. He said it was not fair to the men themselves because people thought them slackers and it was not fair to America. It is awfully hard for Jack to stay there—I know—but such is life—it's nobody's fault—only fate to blame. Maybe, in time, he could get into the Army.

Just think—twenty-seven today!—we are going down to the Canteen for dinner. There will be sixteen of us—Dode is giving the Party, and we are to have Lobster Salad—green peas in butter—French fried potatoes—rolls—coffee—white wine—Real *Ice Cream* with fresh peaches and—I think—a birthday cake.—Oh isn't this a terrible war!!!—After all we heard——

I saw Eleanor Mitchell,[12] of St. Cloud, and Daisy Grey,[13] of Minneapolis, in Paris the other day. I almost fainted when I saw Eleanor. I didn't know she was even considering France. Paris seems very gay now. Everyone is so happy over the turn the war seems to have taken but, at the same time, we are all very cautious about our hopes. No one thinks that we will see the end for at least another year—but even then—that is wonderful!!![14]

---

12. Eleanor Mitchell (1877–) was forty-one years old when she traveled to France in August 1918.

13. This is probably Julia Marguerite Grey (1878–).

14. At this point, many solders and political leaders still expected the Germans to retreat and hold at the Hindenburg Line and that the war would be

Your last letter spoke of us being near the front. Don't worry!! No Red Cross girls are ever within shell-fire. We are safe wherever we are because people are always looking out for us. And besides, the Germans are going in the other direction these days.[15] Even their Air Raids are null and void. We have had only a few warnings in the past weeks and the warnings is all we do have—They never get here for some reason or other.

Well—Good Bye—I must change my shirt for the party—
Love to you all.
Alice

P.S. Please send what money I have in the bank to Morgan-Harjes, Paris. The Merchant's will do it for you.

Dode sends her Love too. I told you that Ruth was not coming didn't I? I am having some requests for things approved and will send them to you when I get them.

～

31 August 1918
[Chantilly]

Dear Mother—

Kindly send me one dozen pairs of black silk stockings, size 10.

Affectionately,
Alice O'Brien

～

concluded in the spring of 1919. Enormous plans for a springtime offensive were being developed. Cruttwell, *History of the Great War*, 547.

15. By the end of August, the Allied troops had pushed the Germans even father back, eliminating all the gains they had made in 1916. Cruttwell, *History of the Great War*, 554.

[~September 8, 1918]
[Chantilly]

Dear Mama & All—

Received a letter from you, Nonie, Budge, and Jack this a.m. so my morale is very high today. Jack wrote that he was coming over with the R.C. and, now that he has made the decision, I am very glad but I am afraid that he will have another disappointment on account of being within the draft age. Mr. Wann[16] couldn't stand the Y.M.C.A. any longer so is now with the Red Cross and is to be stationed near Toul so, when we get there, we hope to see him. We have not decided yet where we will go for our furlough but Mrs. Olds is going with us. We are glad because she is a peach and knows France so well, having been here several times before the War. We think we will go to a quiet little Inn she knows of in Brittany. Mugs wants to see Wally,[17] if possible, but there is not much chance of arranging it. I have not seen any of the Birminghams, would not know them if I did, but if I hear of anyone by that name I shall introduce myself. The typewriter is O.K. but it never seems to be around when I feel like writing. I am at the Canteen now, therefore the stylish paper. I have just finished cutting 150 loaves of bread and 36 cheeses.

Three hours later.

I was interrupted to help with the service. We are short-handed again so, between trips in the Ford, I fill in here and there. We fed 1080 men this noon so you can imagine that there was some rush.

I have had some letters, requesting things to be sent me, O.K.'d in Paris so I will send them to you one by one. Each letter must be shown at the post office with the parcel ready for shipping and they

---

16. Likely Thomas Leslie Wann (1861–).
17. Marguerite Davis's brother Wallace (Wally) Davis.

will accept it. You said that you knew that there were many things I needed but that is really not so. We can buy everything in Paris, even the things I am sending for, but they are very expensive and not always of good quality. I am not sending for shoes as I can get American shoes in Paris, in fact have already bought some at Harmans. They cost 100 francs—(twenty dollars) but "C'est la Guerre." I do not need my fur coat. My leather coat is very warm. Some of the girls have fur coats with them but they said they did not put them on over twice all last winter. Please have Ringold make the flannel shirts that I am asking for, just as he made my last one, collar attached, high collar with pointed ends—like Bob's soft collars—there are some silk shirts in my chiffonier drawer that you can show him. The purple striped one was good. I will enclose a sample—get the flannel as near the color as you can but if not exact it doesn't matter. In case the sample should be lost out of this letter get a blue a little darker than sky-blue. It is the Canteen Dept. color and we wear shirts to match the tabs on our lapels. Get a blue "Vyella" [sic] flannel if you can—not too heavy.[18]

Yes—we wear our uniforms at all times, dinners, etc. In fact we are compelled to wear them so I am glad that we have got a lot of useless stuff with us.

We are looking forward to Toul because we will see hundreds of American boys every day and it will be nice to be with our own again but I do think that we will miss the gratitude and the manners of the French Soldiers. They are so appreciative, patient and nice tempered—They are really a wonderful crowd and just think of their courage and the way they are fighting after four long years. You can not imagine the difference in morale now and when we arrived. When we first came out here the Germans were making their big push, trying to get to Paris, and only seventeen miles away, we could hear the roar of the big guns day and night. Nobody would admit that

---

18. Viyella was a branded blend of wool and cotton.

things looked bad but everyone was strangely unhappy and depressed. But now things are so different. Everyone reads the papers with a smile and the front has been pushed back so far that it is only rarely that we hear the cannon.

Well—we're off for the day and will go home in the Ford—thru several little villages and the Forest of Chantilly, one of the most beautiful places in the world.

Love to you all—will send some Kodaks soon.—Poor Dolly K.— I always forget to mention her when I am writing. You must miss the Browns.

Love again,
Alice
Please have the Merchants' [sic][19] forward my money.

~

10 September 1918
[Chantilly]

Dear Mama & All—

Am going to enclose a picture of us taken the morning Lucile was here and also a picture of our little house. I wonder if we will be half so comfortable in Toul.

Sunday, the anniversary of the Battle of the Marne, six of us travelled over to Meaux in the little Ford, to see the doings and the Battlefield. Both cars were going but the other one had tire trouble, that day of all days, so the Ford was our only remaining conveyance. It was pouring rain so we wrapt [sic] ourselves in rubber coats and started off. We went thru some stunning forests—they are so suprising [sic] because you would expect France to have been logged long ago, past a German Prisoner's camp, little wooden huts with high

---

19. Merchants National Bank, located on East Fourth Street in St. Paul.

barb-wire fences all around, past many aviation fields, met all sorts
of traffic on the road, Convoys, cannons, Ammunition trucks, ambulances, etc, and finally dropped down into the Valley of the Marne
and saw the little town of Meaux, with its beautiful Cathedral, spread
out before us. It all looked so peaceful and quiet that it was hard to
imagine what a hell it was four years ago that day. We first visited the
Cathedral, beautiful tall Gothic arches and columns and all resplen-
dant [sic] with the flags of the Allies. It gave me a thrill to see our Stars
and Stripes hanging over the Altar beside the flags of France and
England. Then we went out to the Battlefield, five kilometres [sic] the
other side of town. The roads and fields were dotted with little groups
of people dressed in black, French families visiting the graves of
their dead soldiers who fell in the Battle and were buried on the
field. That particular part of France resembles the rolling wheat
fields of Minnesota and, as far as your eye could carry, you saw the
tricolored flags of France waving in the breeze, each flag marking
the grave of the man buried there. A large monument marks the
place of the turning point in the Battle and it was weighed down with
wreaths and flowers. We went home about sunset, thru beautiful
country spotted with hay stacks, passed numerous little villages each
with its church spire standing against the sky like a sentinel, saw
aeroplanes in the air looking like huge birds, splashed and bounced
thru the mud and puddles and pulled into Chantilly long after dark,
tired, hungry as bears but delighted with the afternoon we had spent.

We expect to leave here the end of the week but you never can tell
because it takes so much time for papers, passes, etc, Mugs, Dode, a
girl named Larrabee[20] from Amsterdam, N.Y., Mrs. Olds and myself
are going off for a little rest. We think to Brittany.

---

20. Hilda Larrabee served with the Red Cross in France from July through
November 1917, working side by side with Alice in Chantilly for a majority
of that time.

You asked about Church. I get there when I can which is quite regular but when I can't I can't that's all. Last Sunday Mrs. Church and I got up at five-thirty to get to Mass before work but that makes an awfully long day so it isn't always done.

Don't send me shoes. You keep talking about rubber soled shoes— I don't want them. They wouldn't last five minutes on these concrete floors. Besides my feet are O.K. not at all troublesome—never have been.

The enclosed caricature of me was drawn by Mugsy for my birthday party. She drew all the place card caricatures of each one of us and they were killingly funny. I am shown on my return from market, the Ford behind me, and arrayed in my French tam and slicker from Abercrombie's. Isn't it funny? Note the pink shirt.

Love to All,
Alice

P.S. I am enclosing another approved request. Please send them by mail—perhaps registered.

~

21 September 1918
"The White House"
Chantilly, France

Dear Mrs. O'Brien—

The spirit has moved me to write you a letter and I know that you will be glad to have a little side light on Al and her doings "over here."

In the first place, everyone in the Canteen adores her, she is such a good worker and such a good sport. She drives one of our Canteen trucks and besides doing that and all the buying of meat & vegatables

Marguerite Davis's sketch of Alice as a truck driver, made for a place setting for Alice's twenty-seventh birthday, September 1, 1918.

[sic] that goes with it, she turns in and lends a hand in all the other work. Everyone thinks she is a perfect peach.

But I want to tell you that I watch her with an eagle eye and will never let her get tired out. I told you I would take care of her and I will.

My, Mrs. O'Brien, it's lucky that we are both here together or I think sometimes we'd die of homesickness. But when we feel that malady coming on we just sit down together and have a good long talk about home and family and after that relief we feel much better.

I imagine my sister [likes] being all married & settled down in her own house by now—that was one of the biggest shocks of my life & I don't think I will ever get over it. Now that she is not coming over here I suppose we won't be able to get all the things from America that we wanted, but we really can find anything we need right here in France.

Mugsy & Al & I are still waiting for our "releasers," so that we can leave here for our new place at Toul. We are crazy to get a whack at |an American Canteen though nothing will ever be more agreeable than working with these dear old Poilus. And then I don't hesitate to say that we are looking forward to our ten day leave which we will have before going to Toul. It will be some treat, for we have only had two days off in the past fifteen weeks.

Well, I thought you would sort of like hearing a bit more about Al than she would tell you herself, though I suppose she would die if she could read the first part of this letter. I must also add that she is getting quite a little plumper in the face than she was in America.

Now I must to work. With much love to everyone,
Doris

26 September 1918
[Chantilly]

Dear Mama, Dad and All—

We are going to Paris tomorrow and it is such a good opportunity to mail a letter that I don't want to miss it so will dash this off tonight. Mrs. Church is sending one of the Cars in to do the Paris market in the morning so Dode, Mrs. C. and I will stay in over night, get up at four in the a.m. and go to the famous market before dawn. That is the time it is at its height. As it is one of the most interesting places in Paris we are delighted to go and especially as we have buying to do. It is so much more fun than just looking on.

Redfern is making some of the R.C. Uniforms this fall so Dode and I are ordering ones there and will have a fitting tomorrow.[21] We have written to Major & Mrs. Olds to have dinner with us so the five of us will have a very cozy time together. We are still waiting for the new workers to come so we can go on our permission. I hope it will not be delayed too long or Brittany will be cold and damp. Mrs. Olds is going with us and is just as keen as we are for a rest. She works very hard at the R.C. free dispensary for refugees, in Paris, and needs a change. Major Olds is going to join us for the week-end so it will all be very nice if it ever comes off. We are beginning to think that the new workers are myths and that they never will arrive. Mrs. Vanderbilt is going to put people fresh from America at the Canteens for the winter, as she considers it a hard post, especially the Commuting.

Dode and I room together always!! Mugs does live in the house with us—has ever since the second week we were here—we are all so

---

21. Redfern was a couture shop famous for its tailored suits and sportswear. Founded by Englishman John Redfern in 1881, the store had locations in London, Paris, New York, and other cities. Fukai, *Fashion: A History*, 719.

A group of Red Cross women were photographed at a camp in France. Alice, second from right, proudly sports her chauffeur's beret.

comfortable and happy together. Seven tired faces around the dinner table every evening but I must say I wish Mrs. Church wouldn't talk so much about the Canteen and the servants. We would like to forget it by the time we get here, tired and hungry. However, all in all, she is a peach and I only hope the one at Toul will be half as satisfactory. The rest of the girls & women live at the Hotel. One woman, Mrs. English[22] from Denver, came about a month ago, is a scream. She told us that she was very prominent in Denver and expected to chaperon young girls in a Hostess House in France. She expected a snap but she hasn't seen it yet. You would die to see her trying to put in a full days work. She stretches out on the couch at the Canteen like a corpse as soon as her shift is relieved and it's all

---

22. Likely Mary Jackson English (1873–). Mrs. English was one of the few married women to serve as a canteen volunteer with the Red Cross in France.

she can do to crawl to the train. Washington is crazy to let over people of her stamp.

Love to you all—write soon,
Alice

~

30 September 1918
[Chantilly]

Dear Mama, Dad and All—

Just six months ago today we steamed out of New York Harbour. It seems but yesterday that I stood at the window of the Custom House and waved Good-Bye to Mama, Aunt Lorene and Ed. You looked awfully good to me then but how much better you will look as you stand on the pier to welcome us back. Have the whole family there. If Dad doesn't get to New York for that event I will be disappointed. Let us hope that when we cross again the sea will be free of lurking submarines. It is beginning to look as tho that day would really come.[23] Think of the Huns, with all their devilment, defeated. All I ask—and I don't think it too much, is to pull a tooth from the face of the Kaiser. I have my own ideas about doing it too. What do you

---

23. On September 26, Foch declared "Tout le monde a la bataille," and the Allies launched a new offensive at Argonne. Germany's weary, fragile lines fell back again, though not significantly. On September 28, Lundendorff learned that Germany's ally Bulgaria was seeking an armistice with the Allies. Lundendorff suffered an emotional breakdown and told Hindenburg there was no choice but armistice. The following day, the German military and political leaders approached the Kaiser and informed him that armistice was desperately needed and that he would need to abdicate. Keegan, *The First World War*, 412–13; Johnson, *1918: The Unexpected Victory*, 145–46; Cruttwell, *History of the Great War*, 561.

think of this—There is a very well-educated French Boy in C.__, speaks English well and is from a very nice family. His Father is dead and he lived with his Mother and Sister in Northern France. When the war broke out he was called to the Colors and shortly afterwards the Germans invaded the Country and took his Mother and Sister prisoner. He had not heard from them for four years until, one day, he received word that they were to be returned to France via Switzerland. Insanely happy he went to meet them only to find his Mother a broken wreck and his Sister, a girl of eighteen, with her right foot cut off. His eyes filled with tears as he told us about it and he cherishes a bitter hatred against Germany. He said that the story of his Sister was too terrible to relate so you can just imagine what she suffered. No wonder people hate the Germans. I don't think it wrong. I almost consider it a virtue.

We are still waiting for the new workers to come. It is getting cold and if they don't come soon I am afraid the weather will be raw in Brittany. However we are going if we can because it is so restful and picturesque there. The last two times I have been in Paris Major Olds has been out of town but I think he has cabled for Mary[24] and feel sure that he will cable for the Kavanaughs, now that I know they surely want to come. Tell them that the arrangements will probably be that they will sign up with the Military Affairs Department and be assigned to work when they get here. They need stenographers badly but tell them that they may have a chance to sign with the Canteen Dept. and if they get the chance to take it. It's hard work but much the sportiest and most interesting of all the Red Cross work.

Isn't it fine that Bob is going to Pawling?[25] It must be quite a sacrifice for you to let him go—having everyone away—but it is fine for

---

24. Likely Mary Morrissey.

25. Pawling School, now known as Trinity-Pawling School, is an all-boys boarding school located in northern New York.

him. I think that the Pawling boys have fine spirit and it would be nice for him to go right on then till he graduates.

It is beginning to get cold now and the mornings are dark and chilly when we get up at six o'clock and dress by yellow candle light. There is a shortage of coal and it looks like a long cold winter ahead of us. Dode just came into the room and said that I looked like "Biddy with a red nose" so what will I look like when the snow falls. However we are well and fat so have a good start for the winter anyway. Dode is beginning to worry about her figure again and says that she thought there would be no fattening food in France, that's why she came, but Alas! She can't keep away from it. She is at present, standing beside me and soaking her Canteen hands in hot water but their Lily white color will not come back. The Poilus love her ankles and she loves them—She flirts in French so what will she do when we set with the "Yanks."

Well—A French General has just arrived to inspect the Canteen so I'll have to go and see the excitement.

Love to All,
Alice

P.S. I have carried this letter for two days so it is well worn and dirty. Received a letter from you yesterday, written from Eau Claire. Hope the deal went thru. No—I did not receive Dad's letter. I thought perhaps he had disowned me by this time. Ask him to try again—perhaps I'll get the next one. I received one of Mrs. Donnelly's letters and three from Auntie Marie.

Isn't the news wonderful. Everyone expects Turkey to crumble now that Bulgaria has fallen. Next summer will see the finish, I think.

Please don't send my fur coat—I don't want it. I am going to get a uniform coat.

It is awfully interesting here now—every day we see troops and cannon being poured forward to the front and everyone's spirits are high. We feed more and more men each day and the R.C. is going to try to open 45 new Canteens.

Love to you all—wish you were here to see the interesting sights I see.

Alice
Have you forwarded my money to Morgan-Harjes? If not cable it—Did not receive my birthday Cable—Get your money back.

~

6 October 1918
[Chantilly]

Dear Mama and All—

Mugsy is quite delighted today because she has received a letter from her family—the first she has received since they have known that she was not to return this fall. The Red Cross is only too willing to pay people to stay but they always ask if it is necessary for you to receive a salary. Mugs was delighted to accept but Dode and I felt that as long as we could afford to pay our own expenses that we were not justified in accepting money from the R.C. I would rather they spent the money on something else than on me—especially as it is costing me no more to live over here—not as much in fact—as it does at home. Besides, I have never worked for a living and don't want to start making my money on the Red Cross. However, it is different with Mugs. She would have to go home unless she accepted it and the R.C. is only too glad to have her stay on.

Germany, Austria and Turkey have asked for Peace!!![26] Isn't it wonderful!! We yelled for joy when we read the papers this morning.

---

26. On October 3, Prince Max, the new chancellor of Germany, sent a request for armistice to President Wilson. Turkey and Austria soon followed. Johnson, *1918: The Unexpected Victory*, 150–51.

Mrs. Church and I went to Mass at the Convent and when we came out the newsmen were yelling the glad tidings and all the town was agog with excitement. None expect, for a moment, that Wilson will grant what they ask but nevertheless—it is the greatest victory of all to have them humble themselves and beg for it. It shows that they realize their weakness and everyone thinks that it is the beginning of the end. All the French *Officiers* I have talked to laugh at the offer and say that there will never be a satisfactory Peace concluded until the war is pushed back onto German territory. However, all the world waits with abated breaths for Wilson's reply. Whatever the answer, Bulgaria and Turkey are done for and Germany and Austria can't hang on much longer. We'll see the old U.S.A. before long.

Enclosed find a photo of Dode and me taken in the woods, just outside the Canteen, with a group of men who are guards here. Aren't their poses killing? They fixed and primped for half an hour before the event came off. My hands are behind me because they were covered with doughnut dough. They begged us to come but we were so busy we hated to but finally tore out—just as we were—so therefore the result. It was cold so I had my sweater on. Our aprons are Canteen blue—sort of an Alice-blue—and quite good looking. That is to say they were before they were washed a million times. Dode doesn't really look as sick as she seems.

One of the new workers has arrived and we think the rest are soon to follow so perhaps we will move on before long. It will be interesting to be with the Americans after being with the French so long.

Dode and I went to Paris to try on our uniforms and I saw Major Olds. He has cabled for Mary[27] and the Kavanaughs so unless they have spies in their families, or some other sort of buried skeletons, I guess they can come. When they leave St. Paul cable me because I might be in Paris when they come over or could arrange to get there.

27. Likely Mary Morrissey.

Doris Kellogg and Alice O'Brien with poilus outside the canteen at Orry-la-Ville. Alice hid her hands because they were covered in dough.

If they come send pictures of all the family with them. The one of Dad that Howard took, one of your late ones and Kodak pictures of the others if you can't find anything else.—or maybe sometime, when you are all at the House together you could have Howard or someone go there and take you all in a group. I would love it—the whole bunch. Wouldn't it be great. Bob won't be there or perhaps Dad or Jack but the rest of you get yourselves "tooked" anyhow.

Our suits are very nice—fit well and look quite Military but they are older looking than our navy blue ones. However, grey is the Uniform Color so, of course, we have to have it. They are starting a Women's Motor Corps with the Red Cross and I am afraid that they will nab me for it. I would so much rather be a Canteener. It is much sportier and more interesting than driving a car in Paris and if you drive you have to go where they put you whether you like it or not. I heard that G. Washburn[28] has been sent to the South of France to drive. I would hate that.

Well—will close now—Mugs and Dode and some of the others have gone over to the Scottish Woman's Hospital but I was on Duty here and the service (evening) is about to start. We do not have big crowd at night anymore, on account of a change in the train schedule. Love to you all—Have you done anything with or about my Car? What a shame you smashed your fingers—It hurts like sin—I smashed the middle finger on my right hand on a car in Paris when I first came over. I lost the nail but all is well now.

Love again,
Alice

~

13 October 1918
[Chantilly]

Dear Mama & All—

The times are so exciting with these demands for Peace that I cannot settle down to writing a letter. Wouldn't it be wonderful if it were nearly over? But unless the Germans surrender, unconditionally, "on to Berlin."

Four new workers have arrived and another one is expected in a day or so and when she arrives we shake loose. I guess we will go to Brittany after all—we long to. Major Olds cabled for the Kavanaughs and Mary so I hope they are on their way by this time. And I do hope we will be able to see them when they arrive, to hear all the news from home.

---

28. Genevieve Washburn originally traveled and enlisted in the AFFW with Alice, but did not transfer to the Red Cross with her.

I have received the magazines (3) you sent to me but am not getting the New Republic which you said Nonie sent. The mails are so irregular! And when they are large they just scrap the magazines and don't attempt to deliver them.

We are trying to persuade Mrs. Church to leave here and start something with the American Army and all go with her but she seems to be in a rut—stuck here and can't make up her mind to leave. I wish she would because she is quite a peach and should be with the American boys instead of some of the dames that are with them. Did I tell you about the "Hut Mothers"—a bunch of women that were sent over from America to be in U.S. Canteens and when they arrived they took one look at them and sent about 50% packing to America. They were almost decrepit they were so old and a good weeks work in a Canteen would kill anyone of them. I think America must be going mad!

Well—the girls have just arrived—Dode and I came on the early train this a.m.—with the Herald and the abdication of the Kaiser is rumored—I hope it's true.

Well—can't seem to write today—love to all—we are all well—Dode has chilblains in her hands—isn't it queer because it hasn't been cold yet? Poor circulation, I guess.

Love again,
Alice

~

17[18] October 1918
[Chantilly]

Dear Bob, Bobs and Lyman—

Well! So you are all at Pawling and what a happy trio you must make! I remember when I was at school, how I used to hang around the mail box so I thought I would drop you a line from the War Zone.

However, it doesn't seem much like the war zone now because the Huns are being pushed farther and farther back each day and things are getting quiet. When we came here in June, the last German drive was in full swing and only fifteen miles to the North of us so we saw lots of excitement in those days. The Railroads and Stations, bridges, etc., were being bombed every night and we were often awakened by the roar of bombs and felt our little house shake as tho it were going to tumble about our heads. Troops and cannon were passing constantly, detachments of Cavalry trotted thru the streets and all night long heavy cannons rumbled over the cobblestones outside our window but now-a-days we get our excitement by reading the morning papers and when the news is as good as it was this morning, Lille, Douai and Ostend captured by the Allies, it is plenty exciting enough.[29] It is beginning to look as though the end were in view. Won't it be a happy day for the World?

There was an old Poilu in the Canteen last night when the Commandant of the camp came over to tell us that Lille had been taken and when the poor old sail heard the news he burst into tears for joy. His wife and children were captured by the Germans when Lille was taken and he has not heard a word from them for over four years. He hopes against hope that they are alive and well and is going to get a special permission to visit Lille to try and find them or trace of them. This last week has put wonderful spirit into the French and it is a joy to see the beaming faces of the soldiers as they read the papers and realize that after their four long struggling years of war, Peace is in sight. It is too good to be true!

We, Dode, Mugs and I, expect to leave here in a day or two as our furlough is long overdue. We shall go to Brittany for a good rest and then start in at our new post. Toul is over in the Lorraine Sector, quite

---

29. Lille, Douai, and Ostend were taken by the Allies on October 17. Johnson, *1918: The Unexpected Victory*, 161, 168, 173.

near the front, and bids to be a fairly exciting place. That section has been handed over to the Americans so we will see thousands of them every day. It will be fun to be with our own boys and most of them are so delighted to see an American girl that you feel as tho you were helping your Country just to talk to them. Most of them are so lonesome that they try to put on a skit with everyone in skirts so it is not a real compliment to have them fall at your feet. Of course, I like them, and all that, they are nice boys I know and they are lonesome but, after all, one's power of affection is limited and although I am here to do my bit, I think they expect too much at times. However, we always make a stab at anything, so you can imagine me, trying not to look too bored, as I settle down to listen to the family history, hopes and ambitions of some blacksmith from Backwash, Indiana. It's a great life but the sky-line of New York appeals to me more and more and to think of the long, warm, sunny, restful afternoons that I spent on the St. Croix makes me long to get back. Mama "didn't raise her girl to be a worker" and if it were not for the Huns I wouldn't be working—another atrocity to blame them for.

Well—Boys—Have a good time—I hope your Pawling careers will be filled with glory—Square fellows always make good at Boarding School so I expect to find you all Presidents of your respective classes on my return. There are a lot of men dying on the Fields of France for the future of America and the boys in schools today will be the citizens of tomorrow so make hay while the sun shines and remember that in learning to be a credit to a school you're learning to be a credit to the nation.

Vive la France, Vive l'Amerique et bon chance a vous, Lyman, Bobs and last but never, Robert.

Love to you all—be at the dock to meet me when the boat sails in. Alice

22 October 1918

Hotel Continental, 3, Rue Castiglione, Paris

Dear Mama, Dad and All—

Here we are in Paris and at the Hotel that Auntie Marie and Uncle Ed[30] stayed at when they were here. What different circumstances are going on now. The place is filled with officers of all nations and American girls in Uniform. Paris is gay compared to what it was last spring. The Boulevards are crowded with laughing throngs, the flower stalls are filled with all sorts of temptations, the war news is wonderful and 'silver linings are shining thru every cloud.' The only bugbear is the Spanish Flu and that really is quite serious.[31] Three girls were buried at sea from the last passenger ship to arrive from America and 300 men from a convoy. Isn't it terrible? They say that it is more serious in America than it is over here so do be careful all of you. None of the Doctors seem to know much about it but they think it is Streptococi pneumonia. Everyone has been warned to take precautions against it, gargling with antiseptic, etc., and the Authorities are in hopes of getting it under control before long.

Yesterday I experienced one of the biggest thrills since my arrival. Mr. Davison[32] addressed the personnel of the Red Cross and spoke beautifully of the work that was being done, how the Red Cross was expressing the wishes of the American Nation, how a new spirit was coming into the world and how privileged we all were in being able

---

30. Alice's aunt Marie Mullery and her husband, Edward O'Connor.

31. The Spanish Flu was a crisis in both Europe and North America. Nearly a third of all deaths in the American Expeditionary Forces was caused by the flu. The Germans soldiers, suffering worse base health, were even more susceptible, and Ludendorff blamed some of his military failures on the lack of healthy men available. Troops packed into ships were especially endangered by this highly contagious disease. Persico, *Eleventh Month*, 303–4.

32. Henry P. Davison (1867–1922) was chairman of the War Council of the American Red Cross.

to be here and do the work that our hearts are in. After the talks were over all rose and sang the "Star Spangled Banner" and all felt more confident and courageous than ever before. Really the R.C. is a wonderful institution. Think of it. "It is the biggest organization the world has ever known." Think of it. And all founded on money given by the American People. Do you think that, as a family, we have given enough? Remember that we have not suffered thru the war as so many others have and a few hundred dollars doesn't represent the sacrifice of a member of the family. Think it over seriously and give what you can in the next drive, a couple of thousand dollars at least. Sell my car & give the proceeds to the R.C. When I got thinking about the suffering and agony and horror of it all last night, I became so blue that I cried—finally cried myself to sleep I guess—and this morning I wondered if there wasn't something I could do to help more than I am doing. I work as hard as I can, live economically, and try to help financially when I can but not having a private fortune of my own or the capacity for earning one, all I can do is to remind you of it, in case you could forget, and beg you to *shell over* for the next drive.

We are going to the Olds' to dinner tonight and leave for Brittany tomorrow.

We had such a nice talk with Mrs. Vanderbilt today. She said that we were among her best Canteeners and she wished that she had hundreds like us. She starts tomorrow to make a tour of some new Canteens and says that if she finds anything more interesting than Toul she will send us there instead. We will see her on our return to Paris before we go to our new post.

Love to you all—we are looking forward to our rest. I will write you from Brittany.
Love,
Alice
P.S. Mailed a letter to Bob a week ago.

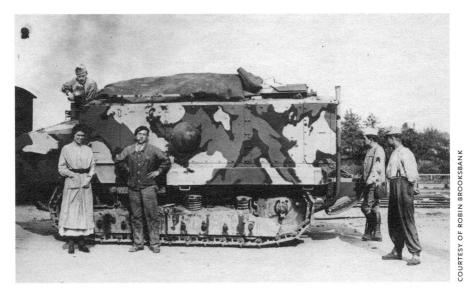

Marguerite Davis with tank, likely at Survilliers.

23 October 1918
Hotel Continental
3, Rue Castiglione, Paris

Dear Lorene—

Just a note before we go to Brittany, we're going tonight, to say that Hilda Larrabee is returning to America in two weeks and is going to call you up on her arrival in N.Y. She has been at Mrs. Church's Canteen with us for the past four months so can tell you all sorts of things in case you care to arrange to see her. She will be in N.Y. for two or three days, would not be able to get to Sea Gate, but if you have nothing better to do you might trot to N.Y., meet her, and get the latest gossip from France. She is a nice girl, we like her a lot, and she is going to Brittany with us for our permission. We all had a wonderfully interesting summer together and she will be able to tell you lots of the details. I told her that Mama will probably make a special trip to Amsterdam, N.Y., that's where she lives, when she hears about it so she is ready for anything.

Paris is wonderful now. The Place de la Concorde is filled with booty captured during the last victorious offensives, Cannon, tanks, rows of Aeroplanes, trench mortors [*sic*], strings and strings of German Helmets and every other symbol of Victory. The City is gay with flags and everyone you see wears a smile on his face.

We are all well but tired so the idea of a vacation looks good to us. On our return we will go either to Toul or to an aviation camp near there.

Love to you all,
Alice

P.S. You spoke of Fords in your last letter. They are wonderful!! France is filled with them and it is a humorous sight to see a tin-lizzie coming down the road, laden down with French generals garbed in light blue uniforms generously decorated with gold braid.

Love again,
Alice

~

[~25 October 1918]
St. John du Doigt, Brittany

Dear Mama and All—

Here we are the five of us in one of the most heavenly places you can imagine. The town is a tiny one and, at present, we are the only strangers in it, in fact, they opened the little hotel to admit us. Madame, the proprietress, told us that she never in the world would have done it unless we were Americans. We are Queens of the place, have a little *salle* with a bright fire blazing all day long and when meal time comes a spick and span maid of Brittany appears, black dress, little white apron, white lace cap and wooden sabots, and lays the covers on a cheerful red checked tablecloth and we gather round the banquet board. And really every meal is almost a banquet. Madame does her own cooking and it is wonderful. French eggs which are a treat as they never serve them in Paris or in any of the canteens any more on account of saving them for the hospitals, fresh butter that would make your mouth water and which even succeeds in making the toasted war bread taste good in the morning with our coffee. We hoped to find a quiet place and we have well succeeded. There are not five hundred people in the settlement, we have not seen an automobile for two days and the only noises we hear are the church bells, an occasional horse and two wheeled cart rumbling over the cobblestones and the soft clatter of wooden shoes on the street. It is so peaceful and quiet and makes a heavenly contrast to the life we have been leading for the last six months. We have resolved not to think or talk about the war but somehow or other we don't seem to always remember and find ourselves in the middle of an earnest discussion before we know it.

The peasants are so quaint, the women with their voluminous skirts, aprons and lace caps and the men with funny trousers and the children looking like pictures out of books. Each little cottage is as immaculately clean as possible and looks good enough to eat with its thatched roof and darling little wall with the hay ricks peeping over. We are about a mile from the sea, just a nice walk, down a little lane lined with old stone houses. The coast line is gorgeous with big black rocks rising out of the bay and the water breaking white all around them. We are going to get an old horse and wagon tomorrow and drive along the beach to a fishing village, watch the fishermen pull in their nets and have a picnic lunch on the beach. The weather is rather dark but the air is soft and makes me think of duck weather in Minnesota. It is a wonderful feeling just to be able to sit and have nothing to do. We are having an orgie [*sic*] of sleep and food and will be in fine shape to start work again.

Mrs. Vanderbilt is now on a tour of inspection and said that on her return she would talk things over with us fully and if anything sounded better to us than Toul she would send us there. They are opening a canteen at an aviation camp near Toul which sounds interesting. The poor boys who have to go out over the lines every day get terribly blue at times and the R.C. is going to try and make life a little easier for them. I should think they would when you consider how short a time most of them have to live.

Paris was in a whirl—filled with booty of all sorts, cannon, aeroplanes, machine guns by the hundreds and everyone as happy and gay as they used to be in ante-bellum days. The city was alive with flags and posters for the fourth French loan, bands were playing, people were buying bonds under the decorated statue of Lille in the Place de la Concorde and they were being sold from a submarine which was anchored in the Seine for the purpose. The last German note was greeted by a general sneer and Peace looks farther off than it did two weeks ago. Opinion seems to be pretty well divided about an early cessation of hostilities some thinking that Peace will surely come before the first of the year and others saying that we might as well settle down for one more year of it. However, there is one thing that everyone agrees on, even Germany, and that is that the Victory will go to the Allies when it does come. Heavens knows when we could get back even if Peace were declared tomorrow but I tell you I won't waste any time about making arrangements when the word comes. Hilda Larrabee is leaving for America in about two weeks and I am going to give her Aunt Lorene's address and she is going to call her up. She has been with us at Chantilly for the last four months so can tell Lorene a lot about things if she can arrange to see her.

We are going down to the ocean this afternoon and are wondering how we are going to get Mitchell[33] there. She is having trouble with a bone in her foot, malnutrition the Doctor said, so can't walk much. We are going to get a little cart and pull her. She says that we are not but we know better. Perhaps a wheelbarrow will fill the bill but we would have to blindfold her to get her into it.

There is an old church and cemetary [sic] just across the street and every morning the bells ring and the people steal out of their houses and clatter to mass. We are going some morning but I do wish that six a.m. was not the popular hour for worship in France. The Church is a very old one and is supposed to contain one of the fingers of St. John, therefore the name of the church and the town, St. Jean du Doigt, meaning St. John of the finger.

Love to all,
Alice

~

26 October 1918
St Jean Du Doigt, Bretagne

Dear Jack—

Quite a time has lapsed since I received your letter with the glorious news that you had been admitted into the army. The end of the war seems to be in sight, I suppose you are already worrying about not getting here, but whatever happens you have done your darndest, finally got in and will have nothing to regret for the rest of your life. I think it's corking!

We are up in Brittany enjoying our rest and permission. Not being used to long days of ease, it has kind of gone to my head and I seem

---

33. Marguerite Mitchell.

to have lost track of things, for instance, it seems to me that I have already written to you to congratulate you on the success of your last great effort which landed you in the army but I can't quite remember whether I did or not so am doing it again. Really, we have been so lazy for the past five days that it is all we can do to remember to eat. And such meals, wonderful! The French certainly know how to cook. They can make anything taste good, even war-time food.

The country around here is wonderfully picturesque with its hills and valleys and little towns nestled in between them. We must bring the family over after the war and tour thru this section. The peasants are just as quaint as characters on the stage and lots of their little houses look as though they had been made of cardboard. We seem far away from the war here yet this place has suffered from it like all others in France. For instance, we went for a drive yesterday, the five of us, in a funny two wheeled cart with a cozy old driver, and stopped at a fishing town near here for luncheon. After the meal we were out in front of the inn talking to the driver and asked him if the town had lost many men in the war and he told us that the Father out of practically every home in the village had been killed. The Bretons make fine soldiers and I guess the Bretons were fairly well wiped out in the beginning of the war when they were thrown in to stop the flow of Germans down the valley of the Marne. Ah well—it will soon be over. They are squealing now and I hope they hold "Thumbs down" on them till every last hun [*sic*] yells out loud for mercy. I think it would be a good thing to condemn the Kaiser to spend the rest of his days in an insane asylum with some of the people whose lives he has ruined.

Well, in spite of my desire to see justice done, sleep seems to assail my mind so I think I shall nap before dinner. We sleep about fourteen hours a day in this establishment but are not sleeped out yet. After working every day for five months without a single day off sleep looks pretty good, especially on these cool mornings.

As soon as we are assigned to our new post I will let you know so when you come over you can let me know and perhaps I could arrange to see you. However, the best address is Morgan-Harjes. Wire me there on your arrival and they will forward it to me wherever I happen to be.

Well, love to all, write soon, be a good soldier and don't get the Spanish Flu. It is quite serious over here but I hear that it is just as bad in America.

Love to all,
Al.

~

1 November 1918, All Souls Day
Still at St. Jean

Dear Mama, Dad and all—

We are still at our darling little Inn and what a glorious time we have had. It has been so restful and quiet, just what we needed, and so homelike. Madame is too good to us. She gives us the best of everything, cooks all sorts of special little things for us, such meals in quantity and quality you have never tasted, and all for the amazing price of ten francs, or two dollars, a day. She and her husband are unexpressibly [sic] grateful for what America has done for France and she is showing her appreciation by treating us like queens. Monsieur went hunting the other day and came home with two partridges which were promptly given to us. We had them for dinner last night, as an entree, we always have two meat courses at each meal, cooked with cabbage in a most delicious way. Eggs are very hard to get but she always manages to find enough to give to us at least once a day. We could not have found a better place in all France to have come to and when you come over, after the war, we will all come here for a day or so.

Yesterday we saw the most thrilling sight. After luncheon, Dode and I started to walk to Plugasnou, a little village about a mile from here. This town is nestled down in a little green valley which stretches to the sea and as we followed the path and climbed the hill we looked out over the sea and there we saw a convoy of camouflaged ships and majestically and watchfully sailing in the sky over head was a huge dirigible airship. The sea was saphire [*sic*] colored, the reflection of light on the dirigible made it a pinkish coral and a brilliant sun threw a golden light over all. It was simply wonderful.

Dode has bought a pair of wooden sabots, a black shawl and a Brittany cap and is all dressed up like a little Peasant. She really looks like the real thing and very sweet and fresh.

Miss Mitchell who was with us has had to return to Paris and is afraid that she will have to go to America. Her foot became very swollen again and she is afraid that it will hang on for a long time. I think her blood is queer because swellings seem to be coming out all over her. Isn't it too bad because she hates to give up and go home. She lives in Brooklyn and if she goes I will tell her to get in touch with Aunt Lorene.

We leave tomorrow afternoon. We drive to Morlaix, twelve miles from here, in an old coach with all our baggage and steamer rugs tucked around us and from there we take the evening train to Paris. We will have time to go to church, get our mail and get into our trunks, etc., etc. before Monday morning when we report at Red Cross headquarters and get back onto the job again. I am keen to get to work and feel so healthy and strong that I look forward to the idea of good hard work.

Today being All Saints Day, we went to mass at the Old village church across the street. The ceremony was very touching especially the part that took place in the Graveyard. I will have to tell you all about it when I get home.

Well, I smell dinner so will close. We heard that Turkey has followed in the heels of Austria and Bulgaria and asked for a separate peace. Things get better every day. Maybe we'll be home for Christmas after all![34]

Love to all,
Alice

⁓

6 November 1918
Paris

Dear Mama, Dad and all the rest—

We are here for a few days before we start for our new post at Toul. We decided to go there as it sounded most interesting. It is right in the heart of the American Sector, just south of Metz, and things ought to be going on there before long. Will write you all about it when we get there.

Spen Kellogg[35] arrived in Paris yesterday A.M. Wasn't it lucky that we were here. It seemed so good to see him and it was such fun hearing all about Ruth's wedding. He is to be assistant chief purchaser of the R.C. headquarters in Paris.

---

34. Negotiations for peace had been going on for nearly a month by this point; Ludendorff had resigned on October 26, and the German military and political leaders were well aware they had lost. They also knew that the peace terms would be more favorable if the Kaiser were removed. Meanwhile, frustrated workers had started to strike in Berlin. The same day Alice wrote this letter, Dr. Wilhelm Drews, the Prussian minister of the interior, met with the Kaiser to attempt to convince him to abdicate. The Kaiser was furious: "The King of Prussia cannot betray Germany. . . . I have no intention of quitting the throne because of a few hundred Jews and a thousand workmen. Tell that to your masters in Berlin!" Johnson, *1918: The Unexpected Victory*, 175–77.

35. Spencer Kellogg, Doris Kellogg's brother.

We reported to the Canteen Dept. yesterday morning and they told me that a Miss Bell[36] was trying to find me so I immediately looked her up. She was at her hotel when I got there so we had quite a talk but I can not say that it was entirely satisfactory. I suppose, knowing that she came direct from St. Paul, I expected too much but our conversation ran about like this:

"Did you see Mama before you left?"

"Yes."

"Was she looking well?"

"Yes."

"Well—what did she have to say?"

"She sent her love."

"Did you see Dad?"

"No."

"Did you see the boys?"

"Yes."

"Were they well?"

"Yes."

(Long silence)

"Well—Did you see Auntie Marie & Teta?"

"Yes."

"Nonie?"

"Yes, they were all well."—etc.—etc.—etc.

It was quite discouraging as I expected to hear loads about you all. However, I invited her to have luncheon with me today so hope to pump something out of her. She did not seem to know that the Kavannaughs [sic] were even thinking of coming over but Major Olds has cabled so I suppose they will be along before long. For heavens sake if they do come tell them to take a good look at every one of you and not to forget the details. Thanks for sending the stockings—

---

36. Grace Mary Bell.

I will call for them at her hotel today. She has been transferred to the Canteen Dept.—lucky I think because the work is more interesting.

I am dying to hear about the Forest fires in Minnesota.[37] Do tell me all about them.

Received your letter in which you told of Jack's departure for Camp. He must of been happy. Thank Heaven things seem about over and our American boys will be able to go home without being entirely shot to pieces. I guess their casualties have been pretty heavy but everyone knows what a big price has to be paid for a Victory.

Mrs. Flemming is in Paris, you remember her I'm sure. She used to be Miss Firsh of the Bennett Faculty. Dode and I went to hear her speak last night and are to have luncheon with her tomorrow. She is fascinating and knows about everything in the world. She is a special, correspondant [sic] so gets all sorts of inside information. She told us the Armistice terms that the Allies have drawn for Germany and they are simply staggering. Germany will be down and out for years and the Huns will have to pinch and scrape to get their indemnitys [sic] paid for generations.[38] I guess if they are contemplating

---

37. The Cloquet fire of October 10–12, 1918, remains Minnesota's worst natural disaster. Alice may have heard about it through the papers or directly from Grace Bell.

38. The terms were fierce, indeed. Economist John Maynard Keynes resigned from the British delegation over the unrealistic and harsh treatment of the Germans. Other diplomats shared similar concerns. Germany's representatives had tried to negotiate for better terms, but losses on the front and political turmoil at home weakened their position. In addition to the staggeringly high reparation costs, Germany had to accept responsibility for causing the war, had to sacrifice all its colonies, and had to limit its army to 104,000 men. As hundreds of thousands of German men returned from war, they faced humiliation, no prospect of military jobs, a crushing economy, and a lot of anger. As Hitler described in *Mein Kampf* (1925), "How each one of the points of the Treaty could be branded in the minds and hearts of the German people until sixty million men and women find their souls aflame with a feeling of rage and shame; and torrents of fire

what they call an "honorable peace" this document, when it is published, will knock the wind out of their sails.[39]

Where is your sense of humour? I did not say that I was offended about the rubber-soled shoes at all. I emphasised [*sic*] the fact that I did not want them because I thought you were worrying about my lack of comfortable shoes and I wanted you to know that I can get all sorts of shoes here and that my feet are O. K. I might of kidded you about them a bit but I was anything but offended.

Just had luncheon with Grace Bell but did not manage to get much juiciness out of her. She is a nice girl and will be a fine canteener. Tell her mother that the trip across must have been what she needed because she looks wonderfully well. I got my stockings and gloves—they are fine—thanks a lot.

It is a rainy, nasty day and I am almost homesick so I guess I'll stop writing and put my mind on something else.

Love to all—write often—and—send some pictures.
Love again,
"Al"

~

8 November 1918
Paris

Dear Mrs. O'Brien—

Your little daughter is not little at all! I saw her yesterday—she was a most radiant vision of health and she's been having the time of her life.

---

burst forth as from a furnace and a will of steel is forged from it, with the common cry: 'We will have arms again!'" Winter and Baggett, *The Great War*, 340–41, 348; Johnson, *1918: The Unexpected Victory*, 183–85.

39. In Berlin, civilians and soldiers were protesting in the streets. Even so, the Kaiser continued to refuse to abdicate, falsely believing he had the

Monday when I registered here I inquired about Alice and was much surprised to find her in town on her way to Toul. So we met, I delivered safely into her hands sundry articles at which she devoutly remarked "Thank the Lord, I can stop darning!" Helen Ruff[40] arrived two days later so I'm sure the supply of hosiery will last a few weeks.

I asked to have my service changed over here to Canteen—a little New York girl and I hoped to be assigned to a seaport, where we can speed our boys home! Won't that sound good?

Alice was awfully eager for news of you, and all the family so don't think she's forgetting home in the least. I believe she'd like to go home only no one here feels it's the thing to do!

Goodbye and please feel assured that Alice is enjoying herself thoroughly, is eating plenty of very good food, is in perfectly splendid health and absolutely no flu in sight!

Best wishes to you all—hope the fires didn't damage you any.

Grace Mary Bell

~

11 November 1918
[Toul]

Dear Mama, Dad and All—

I have managed to dry my eyes and pull myself together to write this letter. I have been crying with joy over the signing of the Armistice!

---

loyalty of his troops and subjects. On November 9, as the Kaiser drafted the notice that he was abdicating as emperor but retaining his role as king, Prince Max announced that the Kaiser had renounced the throne. The chancellorship was passed to Friedrich Ebert, who quickly proclaimed Germany a republic. Cruttwell, *History of the Great War*, 588–89.

40. Helen A. Ruff (1888–) traveled to France to work for the Red Cross in October 1918.

Of course, it is too big a thing to realize that Peace has come after four years of hideous war. All the bells rang at eleven o'clock, the soldiers shouted, and everyone is so happy about it all.

I can't write what I feel but you all feel the same way so you know what it is.

We arrived here yesterday (T—) and find it a fascinating place. Had we arrived a day later we would have missed several exciting things, namely the following. We heard cannon booming and soon discovered that the anti-aircraft guns were firing at a Boche plane almost directly overhead. It was a beautiful, clear day, so thousands of feet over us we could see the German plane shining in the sunlight and the shells bursting all around it. Imagine our excitement when we saw it waver, knew that it had been struck, and a minute later saw it start its tumbling career to earth. It flashed in the sun, as it fell, like a spoon hook on the end of a fish line. Suddenly a white spot seemed stationary in the sky and we realized that one man had extricated himself from the wreck and his parachute was bringing him down a prisoner in the Allied lines. The plane fell so rapidly we could not follow it but for a long time we watched the parachute come serenely down. Both landed only two miles from here. The man in the parachute landed without a scratch but the pilot fell with the plane and was instantly killed. Being in the advanced zone is truly exciting. Well, it's too exciting a time to sit and write. I must go out and shake hands with a thousand Americans at least. Will give this note to a girl to mail in Paris.

Am worried to death about the Influenza in America. For heavens sake be careful.

Love to all,
Alice

FIVE

Alice After the War

Soon after the armistice, Alice began preparations to return to St. Paul. In Toul, she said good-bye to Marguerite Davis, who likely traveled home with her sister Lucile in January 1919. Alice and Doris sailed from Bordeaux on Monday, December 2, on the SS *Lorraine*, and arrived in New York on December 16. She was back in St. Paul in time to celebrate Christmas with her family. Considering her reputation for storytelling, it is likely Alice regaled her extended clan of cousins, aunts, and uncles with tales of her experiences on the front.

On return, Alice soon slipped back into her social life, boating, driving, and suffrage work. Her relationships with Marguerite Davis and Doris Kellogg remained close, and the following June she went out to visit Doris and her family in New York.[1] A few years later, Doris asked Alice to be the godmother to her son Spencer Neale.

In June of 1919, as the men and women who served in France continued to trickle home, the US Congress finally proposed the Nineteenth Amendment, giving women the right to vote. Over the next year, as the states began to ratify the amendment, Alice and her contemporaries must have celebrated—both she and Marguerite

---

1. Alice O'Brien letter to Robert O'Brien, 6 June 1919.

Davis had campaigned for suffrage before the war.[2] In August 1920, the amendment finally passed, but Alice did not retire from political activism. In October, she became Minnesota chairman of the Organization of Republican Women's National Motor Corps, a group that offered the use of their cars to help mobilize speakers and support electioneering work. Alice and her fellow volunteers wore blue felt brassards that sported a white elephant with the letters "G.O.P." on it. Each automobile also displayed a "Harding" sticker.[3]

Though the armbands and "motor corps" title seem dated, charming, and suspiciously ineffective today, they captured the enthusiastic spirit of women like Alice. The chairman of the New York City Republican Women's National Motor Corps, Mrs. Estelle Wise Sheffield, had also been in charge of the Motor Corps Division of the National League for Women's Service during the war, and the overlap between her group, veterans of volunteer work in France, and suffrage activists must have been significant. Sheffield stated that the "automobile method of campaigning" had been very effective, and it was at least appealing to women like Alice.[4]

Alice and her contemporaries were charging into the public and political frontiers with the same determination they had brought to the front in France. Many of these women joined the Women's Overseas Service League, and Alice herself joined in November 1919. Understanding that the venues of power lay not only in public forums but in private spaces, Alice realized that fall that she and other women needed to create a space where women could network and promote ideas. In other words, she wanted to be in the club.

∿

2. "Flying Squad of St. Paul Suffragists Paving Way for Visit of Miss Pankhurst," *St. Paul Sunday Pioneer Press*, 6 December 1914, 1.

3. *New York Tribune*, 4 October 1920; *New York Times*, 4 October 1920.

4. *New York Times*, 24 October 1920.

COURTESY OF ROBIN BROOKSBANK

Soon after the war, Alice was photographed with other women who had served in France. She is in the top row, second from right.

In the fall of 1920, Alice and a group of other St. Paul women met to discuss forming a new club, a place to socialize, share knowledge, work on common projects, lunch, and relax. Though there were many such clubs in St. Paul, they were for men only. Women in Minneapolis had formed a women's club in 1907, but St. Paul did not have such a space. Alice and her friends began recruiting, and in February 1921 an initial meeting drew over 850 women. The attendees agreed to form the Women's City Club of St. Paul, to recruit a thousand members, and to begin fundraising for a future clubhouse. Though by 1924 the club newsletter proclaimed that "The Women's City Club has no political, economic, or social platform," the group itself was clearly committed to promoting women;

as Alice put it, "our power lies in the strength of our 1,000 free-thinking members."[5]

Voting rights and private clubs did not bring equality, as Alice and her friends learned. In the summer of 1921, the national lack of acknowledgment for the service that Alice and other women had offered during the war began to rankle. In June, the Women's Overseas Service League met in Minneapolis to discuss getting congressional recognition for the women volunteers who had served overseas. As the WOSL pointed out at the time, army nurses were the only ones to be given the victory medal for service under fire, while the only nurse wounded was a Red Cross volunteer not entitled to that recognition. In behavior typical of the day, however, the WOSL members unanimously voted to clarify that they would "stand back of the disabled war veterans and help them with their allotments and in job finding"—as if securing the federal government's recognition of the women's efforts would somehow delay disabled men finding jobs.[6]

In the fall of 1921, Alice was ready for a new challenge. She and her friend Katherine Ordway began planning an ambitious trip to Japan, China, Korea, the British East Indies, Java, and Hong Kong, setting sail on the *Empress of Asia* on December 8, 1921.[7] Though records of her actual travels are sparse, it is clear she and Katherine did reach China, Japan, and the Philippines. In China, they met an art historian, Osvald Sirén, and following his advice purchased several paintings, sculptures, and bronzes.[8] Most of these items are now in the collections of the Minneapolis Institute of Arts. Alice and Katherine returned on June 5, 1922.

∽

5. "Alice O'Brien and the Women's City Club of St. Paul," Thomond R. O'Brien, *Minnesota History* 54.2 (Summer 1994): 54–68.

6. *Minneapolis Morning Tribune*, 25 June 1921.

7. Passenger lists, passport applications, and photos document this trip.

8. Conversation with Tomy O'Brien Sr., summer 2007.

But Alice was clearly infected with the travel bug. Over the next decade, she took at least six different overseas trips. In 1923, she went to Europe with her brother Robert. The following year, Alice and her extended family traveled to Europe for the tour she had begun to plan back in 1918. Though brother Jack did not come, Alice, Robert, their parents, and aunts Marie Mullery O'Connor and Teresa Mullery all traveled together. When the rest of the family returned in April, Alice and Marie decided to stay a bit longer. Unfortunately, that was the last time Alice saw her youngest brother. Just weeks later, Robert died in a car crash in Jacksonville. Alice and Marie cut their trip short and hurried home to attend the funeral.

The following year, in 1925, Alice's father, William O'Brien, also died. This loss certainly caused a shift in Alice's life, and it appears that she and her mother gave up their Holly Avenue address and moved permanently to the Marine on St. Croix home. Now thirty-four years old, Alice took a leading role alongside her brother Jack in managing her father's business affairs, which were spread among Minnesota, Florida, and the Carolinas. Alice maintained a business office in downtown St. Paul.

In 1926, Alice traveled to Europe with her brother Jack and his new wife Katherine (Cotty) Smith. The following year, Alice was back again in Europe, this time with her mother and Aunt Marie. Her steamer trunks were barely unpacked when Alice began scheming for even greater adventure: a trip up the Congo River and across the African continent.

For this expedition, Alice needed equally strong-willed companions, and she turned to her close friends, the writer Grace Flandrau and her husband Blair. Alice and Grace had likely met when they were both students at Miss Backus' School for Girls. While Grace had married early, she and Blair never had children, making them available for the types of adventures that most appealed to Alice. When Grace was out of town for her writing commitments, Alice kept company with Blair, partially to enjoy his conversation and partially to watch over his health and drinking.[9]

Ben Burbridge, a big game hunter from Jacksonville, Florida, and Charles E. Bell, a cameraman from St. Paul, also accompanied them. Alice set sail from New York City on the *Aquitania* at midnight on October 26, 1927, and returned on the *Paris* on May 30, 1928. Her six-month adventure was chronicled in the book *Then I Saw the Congo,* written by Grace Flandrau and published in 1929. Alice and Charles Bell edited some 26,000 feet of footage into a feature-length film titled *Up the Congo* and released it in 1929. Though Alice had plans of bicycling across the continent and shooting an elephant, the book and film depict how she, the Flandraus, Bell, and Burbridge traveled by train, boat, canoe, and sedan chairs carried by locals from village to village. They observed dances and daily life and tried their best to ward off serious illness or fatigue of each other's company, with uneven success at the last two.

It was not that unusual for women like Alice to remain single. Though there is little evidence that she was significantly romantically involved with any particular man, one of the few suggestions occurred in a newspaper account of the African trip where Ben Burbridge was described as Alice's fiancé. This status appears unlikely, however, as no other newspaper accounts describe them as engaged. He had been previously married, though possibly separated from his wife during this time period. Whatever the nature of their relationship before the trip, Alice ended it thoroughly tired of his company, and it appears their relationship did not continue beyond their African travels.

When Alice returned to St. Paul from Africa, she focused her energies on the construction of the clubhouse for the Women's City Club. Her fund-raising acumen and publicity stunts proved so successful,

---

9. Ray, *Grace Flandrau,* 169.

the club opened in 1931 without a cent of debt—an incredible accomplishment considering the price of construction and the economic realities of the early years of the Great Depression.

Alice's trips overseas continued: 1930 to France, 1934 to Mexico to visit Grace Flandrau, 1936 to France again. After World War II, Alice's international travel declined. She took one significant trip to France in 1953 with her friend Grace Flandrau, her twin nephews Thomond and Terrence O'Brien, and her newlywed niece Judy O'Brien and her groom, Dick Wilcox.

In these years, Alice settled into a familiar pattern of summers in Marine on St. Croix and winters in a house in Captiva Island, Florida. She often traveled back and forth on her yachts, the *Wanigan I, II, III.* In 1945, Alice donated 180 acres along the St. Croix River to the state of Minnesota in order to establish a park named after her father, William O'Brien. Throughout her life, Alice continued to advocate for causes such as the Children's Hospital of St. Paul, Camp Courage, and surgical research at the University of Minnesota. She worked with the Jay N. (Ding) Darling Foundation in Florida until her death in 1962.[10]

~

World War I changed our world, and it changed Alice, too. Despite the hopes of Woodrow Wilson and others, it was not the "war to end all wars." On the contrary, the peace terms that were established helped build in the economic fragility and promote the types of nationalistic anger that triggered Adolf Hitler's rise. Within a generation, Europe had gone to war again.

In the United States, though, World War I permanently shifted social norms and opened up new discussions of what democracy

---

10. "Miss O'Brien Funeral Set For Monday," *St. Paul Pioneer Press,* 11 November 1962.

and equality meant. Women gained suffrage, and the struggle for African American civil rights and equal treatment drew attention. For both groups, the return to peacetime brought a reevaluation of their roles. The 1920s ushered in economic growth, the birth of jazz, and the rise of the flapper.

Women, especially wealthy ones, began to explore ways to stake their claim to public spaces. In F. Scott Fitzgerald's novels, these wealthy women were beautiful, complex, and often tragic figures, trapped by social expectations and acting out in generally self-destructive ways. They bore little resemblance to pragmatic, progressive, and effective women like Alice and her peers, busy promoting the vote, running charities, and managing large building campaigns.

As the country shifted through the Depression and entered World War II, memories of the contributions of Alice and other volunteer war workers in France had begun to fade. Rosie the Riveter and the Women Airforce Service Pilots became cultural icons of independent women who served the war effort—and were often characterized as "the first" women to do so. Those factory workers and pilots were strong women who challenged barriers during wartime, certainly, but they were not the first.

Women were more than bit players in World War I. They were more than witnesses or victims. And they were more than the gendered stereotypes of feminized nurses, masculinized drivers, or sexualized spies. As Alice's letters show, American women served in France in a variety of ways, and brought the full spectrum of human characteristics with them. Alice herself was a mechanic, an auxiliary nurse, a canteener, and a supply truck driver. She was brave, she was proud, she was jingoistic, she was loyal, she was flirty, she was judgmental, she was funny, she was fearful, she was human, and she was there. Alice and her peers were true actors in World War I, and their stories must not be forgotten.

Bibliography

Primary

American Red Cross Minneapolis. "Northern Division Bulletin" (1918). Twin Cities Red Cross Chapter Archives.

Robin Brooksbank private archives.

Alvina O'Brien private archives.

Helen Scrivers Papers. Manuscripts P362. Minnesota Historical Society.

Dee Smith Papers. Minnesota Historical Society.

Secondary

American Red Cross. *The Work of the American Red Cross During the War: A Statement of Finances and Accomplishments for the Period July 1, 1917 to February 28, 1919*. Washington, DC: American Red Cross, October 1919.

American Red Cross St. Paul Area Chapter. *St. Paul Red Cross Yesterday . . . Today . . . and Tomorrow*. St. Paul Area Chapter, 1976.

Blatch, Harriot Stanton. *Mobilizing Woman-Power*. New York: The Woman's Press, 1918.

Captiva Civic Association. *True Tales of Old Captiva*. Fort Myers, FL: Sutherland Publishing, 1984.

Cruttwell, C. R. M. F. *A History of the Great War, 1914–1918*. Oxford: Clarendon Press, 1934.

Dahl, June Wilkinson. *Footprints: A History of the St. Paul Red Cross*. N.p: American Red Cross, 1981.

Darrow, Margaret. *French Women and the First World War: Stories of the Home Front*. Oxford and New York: Berg, 2000.

Davison, Henry P. *The American Red Cross in the Great War*. New York: The Macmillan Company, 1919.

Dulles, Foster Rhea. *The American Red Cross: A History*. New York: Harper & Brothers, 1950.

Flandrau, Grace. *And Then I Saw the Congo*. London: Harrap, 1929.

Fukai, Akiko. *Fashion: A History from the 18th to 20th Century*. The Collection of the Kyoto Costume Institute. Cologne: Taschen, 2002.

Gaines, Ruth Louise. *Helping France: The Red Cross in the Devastated Area*. New York: E. P. Dutton & Company, 1919.

Gavin, Lettie. *American Women in World War I: They Also Served*. Boulder: University Press of Colorado, 1997.

Graham, Judith, ed. *Out Here at the Front: The World War I Letters of Nora Saltonstall*. Boston: Northeastern University Press, 2004.

Grant, R. G. *World War I: The Definitive Visual History; From Sarajevo to Versailles*. New York: Dorling Kindersley, 2014.

Grayzel, Susan R. *Women and the First World War*. London and New York: Routledge, 2002.

Hansen, Arlen J. *Gentleman Volunteers: The Story of American Ambulance Drivers in the Great War, August 1914–September 1918*. New York: Arcade Publishing, 1996.

Harris, Harvey L. *The War as I Saw It: 1918 Letters of a Tank Corps Lieutenant*. [Minnesota]: Pogo Press, 1998.

Hart, Liddell. *The Real War, 1914–1918*. Boston: Little, Brown and Company, 1931.

Holbrook, Franklin F., ed. *St. Paul and Ramsey in the War of 1917–1918*. St. Paul: Ramsey County War Records Commission, 1929.

Holbrook, Franklin F., and Livia Appel. *Minnesota in the War with Germany*. St. Paul: Minnesota Historical Society Press, 1928–32.

Jennings, J. K. *The Honor Roll of Ramsey County, Minnesota: A Record of Ramsey County's Contribution to the Winning of the Great War*. N.p: 1919.

Jensen, Kimberly. *Mobilizing Minerva: American Women in the First World War*. Champaign: University of Illinois Press, 2008.

Johnson, J. H. *1918: The Unexpected Victory*. London: Arms and Armour Press, 1997.

Johnston, Patricia Condon. *Reflections: The White Bear Yacht Club: 1889–1989*. White Bear, MN: White Bear Yacht Club, 1989.

Keegan, John. *The First World War*. New York: Vintage Books, 1998.

Kellogg, Doris. *Canteening Under Two Flags: Letters of Doris Kellogg*. New York: Roycrofters, 1920.

Kennedy, David M. *Over Here: The First World War and American Society*. New York: Oxford University Press, 1980.

Nelson, James Carl. *The Remains of Company D: A Story of the Great War*. New York: St. Martin's Press, 2009.

O'Brien, Thomond R. "Alice M. O'Brien and the Women's City Club of St. Paul." *Minnesota History* 54 (Summer 1994): 54–68.

Persico, Joseph E. *Eleventh Month, Eleventh Day, Eleventh Hour: Armistice Day, 1918.* New York: Random House, 2004.

Ray, Georgia. *Grace Flandrau: Voice Interrupted.* Roseville, MN: Edinborough Press, 2007.

Scharff, Virginia. *Taking the Wheel: Women and the Coming of the Motor Age.* Albuquerque: University of New Mexico Press, 1991.

Schneider, Dorothy, and Carl J. Schneider. *Into the Breach: American Women Overseas in World War I.* Lincoln, NE: toExcel Press, iUniverse.com Inc, 2000.

Stuhler, Barbara, and Gretchen Kreuter, eds. *Women of Minnesota: Selected Biographical Essays.* St. Paul: Minnesota Historical Society Press, 1977.

Walters, Dorothy V. "Pioneering with the Automobile in Minnesota." *Minnesota History* 26 (March 1945): 19–28.

Winter, Jay, and Blaine Baggett. *The Great War and the Shaping of the 20th Century.* New York: Penguin Studio, 1996.

Index

Page numbers in *italic* refer to images.